Volleyball Score Book

Personal Information

Name: _____

Phone: _____

Address: _____

_____

Email: _____

Book Information

Book Number: _____

Book Start Date: _____

Book End Date: _____

Date:	Location:		Start Time:	Finish Time:

Home Team:	Visitor Team:	Game No.:	Level:

Time-Outs	TEAM:		First Serve	Time-Outs	TEAM:

Running Score

Serve Order	Player No.	Libero # :	Running Score	Serve Order	Player No.	Libero # :
I			1 ¦ 17 1 ¦ 17	I		
			2 ¦ 18 2 ¦ 18			
II			3 ¦ 19 3 ¦ 19	II		
			4 ¦ 20 4 ¦ 20			
III			5 ¦ 21 5 ¦ 21	III		
			6 ¦ 22 6 ¦ 22			
			7 ¦ 23 7 ¦ 23			
IV			8 ¦ 24 8 ¦ 24	IV		
			9 ¦ 25 9 ¦ 25			
			10 26 10 26			
V			11 27 11 27	V		
			12 28 12 28			
			13 29 13 29			
VI			14 30 14 30	VI		
			15 31 15 31			

Substitutions: 1 2 3 4 5 6 7 8 9 10 11 12 13 14 15 16 17 18	16 32 16 32	Substitutions: 1 2 3 4 5 6 7 8 9 10 11 12 13 14 15 16 17 18
Comments:	Final Score	Comments:

REFEREE'S VERIFICATION		SCOREKEEPER	
FIRST REFEREE		WINNING TEAM	
SECOND REFEREE		LOSING TEAM	

KEYS:

C = Playing Captain
S = Substitution
Sx = Substitution Opponent

━| = Loss Of Rally
R = Replay
RS = Re-Serve

T = Time-Out
Tx = Time-Out Opponent
1,2,3..etc = General Point

P1, P2, P3 = Penalty Point
Px = Penalty Opponent
☐ = Point Scored Off Loss Of Rally
△ = Libero Point

If the receiving team wins the rally, it receives a point which is recorded on the line of the next server's number and a square is drawn around it. Also draw a square around the same point on the team's running score. Draw a triangle around serve order position in which the Libero serves and around all points score by the Libero.

Date:	Location:		Start Time:	Finish Time:
Home Team:	Visitor Team:		Game No.:	Level:

Time-Outs		TEAM:	First Serve	Time-Outs		TEAM:
			Running Score			

Serve Order	Player No.	Libero # :	Running Score	Serve Order	Player No.	Libero # :
			1 17 1 17			
			2 18 2 18			
I			3 19 3 19	I		
			4 20 4 20			
II			5 21 5 21	II		
			6 22 6 22			
III			7 23 7 23	III		
			8 24 8 24			
IV			9 25 9 25	IV		
			10 26 10 26			
V			11 27 11 27	V		
			12 28 12 28			
VI			13 29 13 29	VI		
			14 30 14 30			
			15 31 15 31			

Substitutions: 1 2 3 4 5 6 7 8 9 10 11 12 13 14 15 16 17 18   16 32 16 32   Substitutions: 1 2 3 4 5 6 7 8 9 10 11 12 13 14 15 16 17 18

Comments: Final Score   Comments:

REFEREE'S VERIFICATION		SCOREKEEPER	
FIRST REFEREE		WINNING TEAM	
SECOND REFEREE		LOSING TEAM	

KEYS:

C = Playing Captain   ⊣ = Loss Of Rally   T = Time-Out   P1, P2, P3 = Penalty Point

S = Substitution   R = Replay   Tx = Time-Out Opponent   Px = Penalty Opponent

Sx = Substitution Opponent   RS = Re-Serve   1,2,3..etc = General Point   ☐ = Point Scored Off Loss Of Rally

△ = Libero Point

If the receiving team wins the rally, it receives a point which is recorded on the line of the next server's number and a square is drawn around it. Also draw a square around the same point on the team's running score. Draw a triangle around serve order position in which the Libero serves and around all points score by the Libero.

| Date: | | Location: | | | | | | Start Time: | | Finish Time: | |

| Home Team: | | Visitor Team: | | | | Game No.: | | Level: | |

| | Time-Outs | TEAM: | | | | First Serve | | Time-Outs | | TEAM: | |

Running Score

Serve Order	Player No.	Libero # :			1 17 1 17	Serve Order	Player No.	Libero # :
					2 18 2 18			
I					3 19 3 19	I		
					4 20 4 20			
II					5 21 5 21	II		
					6 22 6 22			
III					7 23 7 23	III		
					8 24 8 24			
IV					9 25 9 25	IV		
					10 26 10 26			
V					11 27 11 27	V		
					12 28 12 28			
					13 29 13 29			
VI					14 30 14 30	VI		
					15 31 15 31			

| Substitutions: 1 2 3 4 5 6 7 8 9 10 11 12 13 14 15 16 17 18 | 16 32 16 32 | Substitutions: 1 2 3 4 5 6 7 8 9 10 11 12 13 14 15 16 17 18 |
| Comments: | Final Score | Comments: |

REFEREE'S VERIFICATION		SCOREKEEPER	
FIRST REFEREE		WINNING TEAM	
SECOND REFEREE		LOSING TEAM	

KEYS:

C = Playing Captain
S = Substitution
Sx = Substitution Opponent

—| = Loss Of Rally
R = Replay
RS = Re-Serve

T = Time-Out
Tx = Time-Out Opponent
1,2,3..etc = General Point

P1, P2, P3 = Penalty Point
Px = Penalty Opponent
☐ = Point Scored Off Loss Of Rally
△ = Libero Point

If the receiving team wins the rally, it receives a point which is recorded on the line of the next server's number and a square is drawn around it. Also draw a square around the same point on the team's running score. Draw a triangle around serve order position in which the Libero serves and around all points score by the Libero.

Date:	Location:		Start Time:	Finish Time:
Home Team:	Visitor Team:		Game No.:	Level:

Time-Outs	TEAM:	First Serve	Time-Outs	TEAM:

Running Score

Serve Order	Player No.	Libero # :									1 17 1 17	Serve Order	Player No.	Libero # :									
I											2 18 2 18	I											
											3 19 3 19												
											4 20 4 20												
II											5 21 5 21	II											
											6 22 6 22												
III											7 23 7 23	III											
											8 24 8 24												
IV											9 25 9 25	IV											
											10 26 10 26												
V											11 27 11 27	V											
											12 28 12 28												
											13 29 13 29												
VI											14 30 14 30	VI											
											15 31 15 31												

Substitutions: 1 2 3 4 5 6 7 8 9 10 11 12 13 14 15 16 17 18 | 16 32 16 32 | Substitutions: 1 2 3 4 5 6 7 8 9 10 11 12 13 14 15 16 17 18

Comments: | Final Score | Comments:

REFEREE'S VERIFICATION		SCOREKEEPER	
FIRST REFEREE		WINNING TEAM	
SECOND REFEREE		LOSING TEAM	

KEYS:

C = Playing Captain
S = Substitution
Sx = Substitution Opponent

▬| = Loss Of Rally
R = Replay
RS = Re-Serve

T = Time-Out
Tx = Time-Out Opponent
1,2,3..etc = General Point

P1, P2, P3 = Penalty Point
Px = Penalty Opponent
☐ = Point Scored Off Loss Of Rally
△ = Libero Point

If the receiving team wins the rally, it receives a point which is recorded on the line of the next server's number and a square is drawn around it. Also draw a square around the same point on the team's running score. Draw a triangle around serve order position in which the Libero serves and around all points score by the Libero.

Date:		Location:					Start Time:		Finish Time:	

Home Team:	Visitor Team:	Game No.:	Level:

Time-Outs		TEAM:			First Serve		Time-Outs		TEAM:	

Running Score

Serve Order	Player No.	Libero # :		1 17 1 17	Serve Order	Player No.	Libero # :
				2 18 2 18			
I				3 19 3 19	I		
				4 20 4 20			
II				5 21 5 21	II		
				6 22 6 22			
III				7 23 7 23	III		
				8 24 8 24			
IV				9 25 9 25	IV		
				10 26 10 26			
V				11 27 11 27	V		
				12 28 12 28			
				13 29 13 29			
VI				14 30 14 30	VI		
				15 31 15 31			

Substitutions:1 2 3 4 5 6 7 8 9 10 11 12 13 14 15 16 17 18	16 32 16 32	Substitutions:1 2 3 4 5 6 7 8 9 10 11 12 13 14 15 16 17 18
Comments:	Final Score	Comments:

REFEREE'S VERIFICATION		SCOREKEEPER	
FIRST REFEREE		WINNING TEAM	
SECOND REFEREE		LOSING TEAM	

KEYS:

C = Playing Captain

S = Substitution

Sx = Substitution Opponent

⊣ = Loss Of Rally

R = Replay

RS = Re-Serve

T = Time-Out

Tx = Time-Out Opponent

1,2,3..etc = General Point

P1, P2, P3 = Penalty Point

Px = Penalty Opponent

☐ = Point Scored Off Loss Of Rally

△ = Libero Point

If the receiving team wins the rally, it receives a point which is recorded on the line of the next server's number and a square is drawn around it. Also draw a square around the same point on the team's running score. Draw a triangle around serve order position in which the Libero serves and around all points score by the Libero.

Date:		Location:				Start Time:		Finish Time:	

Home Team:		Visitor Team:			Game No.:		Level:	

Time-Outs		TEAM:		First Serve	Time-Outs		TEAM:	

Running Score

Serve Order	Player No.	Libero # :		1 17	1 17	Serve Order	Player No.	Libero # :
				2 18	2 18			
I				3 19	3 19	I		
				4 20	4 20			
II				5 21	5 21	II		
				6 22	6 22			
III				7 23	7 23	III		
				8 24	8 24			
IV				9 25	9 25	IV		
				10 26	10 26			
V				11 27	11 27	V		
				12 28	12 28			
				13 29	13 29			
VI				14 30	14 30	VI		
				15 31	15 31			

Substitutions: 1 2 3 4 5 6 7 8 9 10 11 12 13 14 15 16 17 18 | 16 32 | 16 32 | Substitutions: 1 2 3 4 5 6 7 8 9 10 11 12 13 14 15 16 17 18

Comments:		Final Score	Comments:

REFEREE'S VERIFICATION		SCOREKEEPER	
FIRST REFEREE		WINNING TEAM	
SECOND REFEREE		LOSING TEAM	

KEYS:

C = Playing Captain
S = Substitution
Sx = Substitution Opponent

⊣ = Loss Of Rally
R = Replay
RS = Re-Serve

T = Time-Out
Tx = Time-Out Opponent
1,2,3..etc = General Point

P1, P2, P3 = Penalty Point
Px = Penalty Opponent
☐ = Point Scored Off Loss Of Rally
△ = Libero Point

If the receiving team wins the rally, it receives a point which is recorded on the line of the next server's number and a square is drawn around it. Also draw a square around the same point on the team's running score. Draw a triangle around serve order position in which the Libero serves and around all points score by the Libero.

Date:	Location:		Start Time:	Finish Time:

Home Team: Visitor Team: Game No.:   Level:

Time-Outs	TEAM:		First Serve		Time-Outs	TEAM:	
			Running Score				

Serve Order	Player No.	Libero # :	1	17	1	17	Serve Order	Player No.	Libero # :
			2	18	2	18			
I			3	19	3	19	I		
			4	20	4	20			
II			5	21	5	21	II		
			6	22	6	22			
III			7	23	7	23	III		
			8	24	8	24			
IV			9	25	9	25	IV		
			10	26	10	26			
V			11	27	11	27	V		
			12	28	12	28			
			13	29	13	29			
VI			14	30	14	30	VI		
			15	31	15	31			

Substitutions: 1 2 3 4 5 6 7 8 9 10 11 12 13 14 15 16 17 18 | 16 | 32 | 16 | 32 | Substitutions: 1 2 3 4 5 6 7 8 9 10 11 12 13 14 15 16 17 18

Comments: **Final Score**   Comments:

REFEREE'S VERIFICATION		SCOREKEEPER	
FIRST REFEREE		WINNING TEAM	
SECOND REFEREE		LOSING TEAM	

KEYS:

C = Playing Captain   ⊣ = Loss Of Rally   T = Time-Out   P1, P2, P3 = Penalty Point

S = Substitution   R = Replay   Tx = Time-Out Opponent   Px = Penalty Opponent

Sx = Substitution Opponent   RS = Re-Serve   1,2,3..etc = General Point   □ = Point Scored Off Loss Of Rally

△ = Libero Point

If the receiving team wins the rally, it receives a point which is recorded on the line of the next server's number and a square is drawn around it. Also draw a square around the same point on the team's running score. Draw a triangle around serve order position in which the Libero serves and around all points score by the Libero.

Date:	Location:		Start Time:	Finish Time:
Home Team:	Visitor Team:		Game No.:	Level:

Time-Outs	TEAM:		First Serve	Time-Outs	TEAM:	

Running Score

Serve Order	Player No.	Libero # :		1 17 1 17	Serve Order	Player No.	Libero # :
				2 18 2 18			
I				3 19 3 19	I		
				4 20 4 20			
II				5 21 5 21	II		
				6 22 6 22			
III				7 23 7 23	III		
				8 24 8 24			
				9 25 9 25			
IV				10 26 10 26	IV		
				11 27 11 27			
V				12 28 12 28	V		
				13 29 13 29			
VI				14 30 14 30	VI		
				15 31 15 31			

Substitutions: 1 2 3 4 5 6 7 8 9 10 11 12 13 14 15 16 17 18 | 16 32 16 32 | **Substitutions:** 1 2 3 4 5 6 7 8 9 10 11 12 13 14 15 16 17 18

Comments: | Final Score | **Comments:**

REFEREE'S VERIFICATION		SCOREKEEPER	
FIRST REFEREE		WINNING TEAM	
SECOND REFEREE		LOSING TEAM	

KEYS:

C = Playing Captain

S = Substitution

Sx = Substitution Opponent

—| = Loss Of Rally

R = Replay

RS = Re-Serve

T = Time-Out

Tx = Time-Out Opponent

1,2,3..etc = General Point

P1, P2, P3 = Penalty Point

Px = Penalty Opponent

☐ = Point Scored Off Loss Of Rally

△ = Libero Point

If the receiving team wins the rally, it receives a point which is recorded on the line of the next server's number and a square is drawn around it. Also draw a square around the same point on the team's running score. Draw a triangle around serve order position in which the Libero serves and around all points score by the Libero.

Date:	Location:		Start Time:	Finish Time:
Home Team:	Visitor Team:		Game No.:	Level:

Time-Outs		TEAM:	First Serve	Time-Outs		TEAM:

Running Score

Serve Order	Player No.	Libero # :									1 : 17	1 : 17	Serve Order	Player No.	Libero # :								
											2 : 18	2 : 18											
I											3 : 19	3 : 19	I										
											4 : 20	4 : 20											
II											5 : 21	5 : 21	II										
											6 : 22	6 : 22											
III											7 : 23	7 : 23	III										
											8 : 24	8 : 24											
IV											9 : 25	9 : 25	IV										
											10 : 26	10 : 26											
V											11 : 27	11 : 27	V										
											12 : 28	12 : 28											
											13 : 29	13 : 29											
VI											14 : 30	14 : 30	VI										
											15 : 31	15 : 31											

Substitutions: 1 2 3 4 5 6 7 8 9 10 11 12 13 14 15 16 17 18 | 16 : 32 | 16 : 32 | Substitutions: 1 2 3 4 5 6 7 8 9 10 11 12 13 14 15 16 17 18

Comments: | Final Score | Comments:

REFEREE'S VERIFICATION		SCOREKEEPER	
FIRST REFEREE		WINNING TEAM	
SECOND REFEREE		LOSING TEAM	

KEYS:

C = Playing Captain
S = Substitution
Sx = Substitution Opponent

⊣ = Loss Of Rally
R = Replay
RS = Re-Serve

T = Time-Out
Tx = Time-Out Opponent
1,2,3..etc = General Point

P1, P2, P3 = Penalty Point
Px = Penalty Opponent
▢ = Point Scored Off Loss Of Rally
△ = Libero Point

If the receiving team wins the rally, it receives a point which is recorded on the line of the next server's number and a square is drawn around it. Also draw a square around the same point on the team's running score. Draw a triangle around serve order position in which the Libero serves and around all points score by the Libero.

Date:	Location:		Start Time:	Finish Time:
Home Team:	Visitor Team:		Game No.:	Level:

Time-Outs		TEAM:		First Serve		Time-Outs		TEAM:	
				Running Score					
Serve Order	Player No.	Libero # :		1 | 17 | 1 | 17		Serve Order	Player No.	Libero # :	
I				2 | 18 | 2 | 18 3 | 19 | 3 | 19 4 | 20 | 4 | 20		I			
II				5 | 21 | 5 | 21 6 | 22 | 6 | 22		II			
III				7 | 23 | 7 | 23 8 | 24 | 8 | 24		III			
IV				9 | 25 | 9 | 25 10 | 26 | 10 | 26		IV			
V				11 | 27 | 11 | 27 12 | 28 | 12 | 28 13 | 29 | 13 | 29		V			
VI				14 | 30 | 14 | 30 15 | 31 | 15 | 31		VI			

Substitutions: 1 2 3 4 5 6 7 8 9 10 11 12 13 14 15 16 17 18 | 16 \| 32 \| 16 \| 32 | Substitutions: 1 2 3 4 5 6 7 8 9 10 11 12 13 14 15 16 17 18

Comments: | Final Score | Comments:

REFEREE'S VERIFICATION		SCOREKEEPER	
FIRST REFEREE		WINNING TEAM	
SECOND REFEREE		LOSING TEAM	

KEYS:

C = Playing Captain
S = Substitution
Sx = Substitution Opponent

⊣ = Loss Of Rally
R = Replay
RS = Re-Serve

T = Time-Out
Tx = Time-Out Opponent
1,2,3..etc = General Point

P1, P2, P3 = Penalty Point
Px = Penalty Opponent
☐ = Point Scored Off Loss Of Rally
△ = Libero Point

If the receiving team wins the rally, it receives a point which is recorded on the line of the next server's number and a square is drawn around it. Also draw a square around the same point on the team's running score. Draw a triangle around serve order position in which the Libero serves and around all points score by the Libero.

Date:		Location:					Start Time:		Finish Time:	

Home Team:		Visitor Team:		Game No.:		Level:

Time-Outs		TEAM:		First Serve		Time-Outs		TEAM:

Running Score

Serve Order	Player No.	Libero # :	1 17 1 17	Serve Order	Player No.	Libero # :
			2 18 2 18			
I			3 19 3 19	I		
			4 20 4 20			
II			5 21 5 21	II		
			6 22 6 22			
III			7 23 7 23	III		
			8 24 8 24			
IV			9 25 9 25	IV		
			10 26 10 26			
V			11 27 11 27	V		
			12 28 12 28			
			13 29 13 29			
VI			14 30 14 30	VI		
			15 31 15 31			

Substitutions: 1 2 3 4 5 6 7 8 9 10 11 12 13 14 15 16 17 18	16 32 16 32	Substitutions: 1 2 3 4 5 6 7 8 9 10 11 12 13 14 15 16 17 18
Comments:	Final Score	Comments:

REFEREE'S VERIFICATION		SCOREKEEPER	
FIRST REFEREE		WINNING TEAM	
SECOND REFEREE		LOSING TEAM	

KEYS:

C = Playing Captain
S = Substitution
Sx = Substitution Opponent

⊣ = Loss Of Rally
R = Replay
RS = Re-Serve

T = Time-Out
Tx = Time-Out Opponent
1,2,3..etc = General Point

P1, P2, P3 = Penalty Point
Px = Penalty Opponent
▢ = Point Scored Off Loss Of Rally
△ = Libero Point

If the receiving team wins the rally, it receives a point which is recorded on the line of the next server's number and a square is drawn around it. Also draw a square around the same point on the team's running score. Draw a triangle around serve order position in which the Libero serves and around all points score by the Libero.

Date:		Location:						Start Time:		Finish Time:	
Home Team:			Visitor Team:					Game No.:		Level:	

<table>
<tr><td colspan="2">Time-Outs</td><td rowspan="2">TEAM:</td><td colspan="2">First
Serve</td><td colspan="2">Time-Outs</td><td rowspan="2">TEAM:</td></tr>
<tr><td></td><td></td><td colspan="2">Running Score</td><td></td><td></td></tr>
<tr><td>Serve Order</td><td>Player No.</td><td>Libero # :</td><td>1 17
2 18</td><td>1 17
2 18</td><td>Serve Order</td><td>Player No.</td><td>Libero # :</td></tr>
<tr><td>I</td><td></td><td></td><td>3 19
4 20</td><td>3 19
4 20</td><td>I</td><td></td><td></td></tr>
<tr><td>II</td><td></td><td></td><td>5 21
6 22</td><td>5 21
6 22</td><td>II</td><td></td><td></td></tr>
<tr><td>III</td><td></td><td></td><td>7 23
8 24</td><td>7 23
8 24</td><td>III</td><td></td><td></td></tr>
<tr><td>IV</td><td></td><td></td><td>9 25
10 26</td><td>9 25
10 26</td><td>IV</td><td></td><td></td></tr>
<tr><td>V</td><td></td><td></td><td>11 27
12 28</td><td>11 27
12 28</td><td>V</td><td></td><td></td></tr>
<tr><td>VI</td><td></td><td></td><td>13 29
14 30
15 31</td><td>13 29
14 30
15 31</td><td>VI</td><td></td><td></td></tr>
<tr><td colspan="3">Substitutions:1 2 3 4 5 6 7 8 9 10 11 12 13 14 15 16 17 18</td><td>16 32</td><td>16 32</td><td colspan="3">Substitutions:1 2 3 4 5 6 7 8 9 10 11 12 13 14 15 16 17 18</td></tr>
<tr><td colspan="3">Comments:</td><td colspan="2">Final Score</td><td colspan="3">Comments:</td></tr>
</table>

REFEREE'S VERIFICATION		SCOREKEEPER	
FIRST REFEREE		WINNING TEAM	
SECOND REFEREE		LOSING TEAM	

KEYS:

C = Playing Captain
S = Substitution
Sx = Substitution Opponent

▬| = Loss Of Rally
R = Replay
RS = Re-Serve

T = Time-Out
Tx = Time-Out Opponent
1,2,3..etc = General Point

P1, P2, P3 = Penalty Point
Px = Penalty Opponent
☐ = Point Scored Off Loss Of Rally
△ = Libero Point

If the receiving team wins the rally, it receives a point which is recorded on the line of the next server's number and a square is drawn around it. Also draw a square around the same point on the team's running score. Draw a triangle around serve order position in which the Libero serves and around all points score by the Libero.

Date:		Location:				Start Time:		Finish Time:	
Home Team:			Visitor Team:			Game No.:		Level:	

Time-Outs		TEAM:		First Serve	Time-Outs		TEAM:	

Running Score

Serve Order	Player No.	Libero # :		First Serve Running Score	Serve Order	Player No.	Libero # :

First Serve column running score:

1 17 1 17
2 18 2 18
3 19 3 19
4 20 4 20
5 21 5 21
6 22 6 22
7 23 7 23
8 24 8 24
9 25 9 25
10 26 10 26
11 27 11 27
12 28 12 28
13 29 13 29
14 30 14 30
15 31 15 31
16 32 16 32

Serve Order left: I, II, III, IV, V, VI
Serve Order right: I, II, III, IV, V, VI

Substitutions: 1 2 3 4 5 6 7 8 9 10 11 12 13 14 15 16 17 18   **Substitutions:** 1 2 3 4 5 6 7 8 9 10 11 12 13 14 15 16 17 18

Comments: Final Score   **Comments:**

REFEREE'S VERIFICATION		SCOREKEEPER	
FIRST REFEREE		WINNING TEAM	
SECOND REFEREE		LOSING TEAM	

KEYS:

C = Playing Captain   ⊣ = Loss Of Rally   T = Time-Out   P1, P2, P3 = Penalty Point

S = Substitution   R = Replay   Tx = Time-Out Opponent   Px = Penalty Opponent

Sx = Substitution Opponent   RS = Re-Serve   1,2,3..etc = General Point   ☐ = Point Scored Off Loss Of Rally

△ = Libero Point

If the receiving team wins the rally, it receives a point which is recorded on the line of the next server's number and a square is drawn around it. Also draw a square around the same point on the team's running score. Draw a triangle around serve order position in which the Libero serves and around all points score by the Libero.

Date:	Location:		Start Time:	Finish Time:
Home Team:		Visitor Team:	Game No.:	Level:

Time-Outs	TEAM:		First Serve	Time-Outs	TEAM:

Running Score

Serve Order	Player No.	Libero # :		1 17 1 17	Serve Order	Player No.	Libero # :
				2 18 2 18			
I				3 19 3 19	I		
				4 20 4 20			
II				5 21 5 21	II		
				6 22 6 22			
III				7 23 7 23	III		
				8 24 8 24			
IV				9 25 9 25	IV		
				10 26 10 26			
V				11 27 11 27	V		
				12 28 12 28			
VI				13 29 13 29	VI		
				14 30 14 30			
				15 31 15 31			

Substitutions: 1 2 3 4 5 6 7 8 9 10 11 12 13 14 15 16 17 18	16 32 16 32	Substitutions: 1 2 3 4 5 6 7 8 9 10 11 12 13 14 15 16 17 18
Comments:	Final Score	Comments:

REFEREE'S VERIFICATION		SCOREKEEPER	
FIRST REFEREE		WINNING TEAM	
SECOND REFEREE		LOSING TEAM	

KEYS:

C = Playing Captain   ⊣ = Loss Of Rally   T = Time-Out   P1, P2, P3 = Penalty Point

S = Substitution   R = Replay   Tx = Time-Out Opponent   Px = Penalty Opponent

Sx = Substitution Opponent   RS = Re-Serve   1,2,3..etc = General Point   ☐ = Point Scored Off Loss Of Rally

△ = Libero Point

If the receiving team wins the rally, it receives a point which is recorded on the line of the next server's number and a square is drawn around it. Also draw a square around the same point on the team's running score. Draw a triangle around serve order position in which the Libero serves and around all points score by the Libero.

| Date: | | Location: | | | | | | | Start Time: | | Finish Time: | |

| Home Team: | | Visitor Team: | | | | | | Game No.: | | Level: | |

| Time-Outs | | TEAM: | | | | First Serve | | Time-Outs | | TEAM: | |

Running Score

Serve Order	Player No.	Libero # :					1 17	1 17	Serve Order	Player No.	Libero # :					
							2 18	2 18								
I							3 19	3 19	I							
							4 20	4 20								
II							5 21	5 21	II							
							6 22	6 22								
III							7 23	7 23	III							
							8 24	8 24								
IV							9 25	9 25	IV							
							10 26	10 26								
V							11 27	11 27	V							
							12 28	12 28								
							13 29	13 29								
VI							14 30	14 30	VI							
							15 31	15 31								

| Substitutions: 1 2 3 4 5 6 7 8 9 10 11 12 13 14 15 16 17 18 | 16 32 | 16 32 | Substitutions: 1 2 3 4 5 6 7 8 9 10 11 12 13 14 15 16 17 18 |

| Comments: | Final Score | | Comments: |

REFEREE'S VERIFICATION		SCOREKEEPER	
FIRST REFEREE		WINNING TEAM	
SECOND REFEREE		LOSING TEAM	

KEYS:

C = Playing Captain
S = Substitution
Sx = Substitution Opponent

⌐| = Loss Of Rally
R = Replay
RS = Re-Serve

T = Time-Out
Tx = Time-Out Opponent
1,2,3..etc = General Point

P1, P2, P3 = Penalty Point
Px = Penalty Opponent
☐ = Point Scored Off Loss Of Rally
△ = Libero Point

If the receiving team wins the rally, it receives a point which is recorded on the line of the next server's number and a square is drawn around it. Also draw a square around the same point on the team's running score. Draw a triangle around serve order position in which the Libero serves and around all points score by the Libero.

Date:		Location:								Start Time:		Finish Time:	
Home Team:			Visitor Team:							Game No.:		Level:	

Time-Outs		TEAM:			First Serve		Time-Outs		TEAM:	
					Running Score					

Serve Order	Player No.	Libero # :							1 17	1 17	Serve Order	Player No.	Libero # :				
									2 18	2 18							
I									3 19	3 19	I						
									4 20	4 20							
II									5 21	5 21	II						
									6 22	6 22							
III									7 23	7 23	III						
									8 24	8 24							
IV									9 25	9 25	IV						
									10 26	10 26							
V									11 27	11 27	V						
									12 28	12 28							
									13 29	13 29							
VI									14 30	14 30	VI						
									15 31	15 31							

Substitutions: 1 2 3 4 5 6 7 8 9 10 11 12 13 14 15 16 17 18 | 16 32 | 16 32 | Substitutions: 1 2 3 4 5 6 7 8 9 10 11 12 13 14 15 16 17 18

Comments: | Final Score | Comments:

REFEREE'S VERIFICATION		SCOREKEEPER	
FIRST REFEREE		WINNING TEAM	
SECOND REFEREE		LOSING TEAM	

KEYS:

C = Playing Captain

S = Substitution

Sx = Substitution Opponent

▬| = Loss Of Rally

R = Replay

RS = Re-Serve

T = Time-Out

Tx = Time-Out Opponent

1,2,3..etc = General Point

P1, P2, P3 = Penalty Point

Px = Penalty Opponent

☐ = Point Scored Off Loss Of Rally

△ = Libero Point

If the receiving team wins the rally, it receives a point which is recorded on the line of the next server's number and a square is drawn around it. Also draw a square around the same point on the team's running score. Draw a triangle around serve order position in which the Libero serves and around all points score by the Libero.

Date:	Location:		Start Time:	Finish Time:
Home Team:	Visitor Team:		Game No.:	Level:

Time-Outs		TEAM:									First Serve			Time-Outs		TEAM:								
											Running Score														
Serve Order	Player No.	Libero # :									1 17	1 17	Serve Order	Player No.	Libero # :									
											2 18	2 18												
I											3 19	3 19	I											
											4 20	4 20												
II											5 21	5 21	II											
											6 22	6 22												
III											7 23	7 23	III											
											8 24	8 24												
IV											9 25	9 25	IV											
											10 26	10 26												
V											11 27	11 27	V											
											12 28	12 28												
											13 29	13 29												
VI											14 30	14 30	VI											
											15 31	15 31												

Substitutions:1 2 3 4 5 6 7 8 9 10 11 12 13 14 15 16 17 18	16 32	16 32	Substitutions:1 2 3 4 5 6 7 8 9 10 11 12 13 14 15 16 17 18
Comments:	Final Score		Comments:

REFEREE'S VERIFICATION		SCOREKEEPER	
FIRST REFEREE		WINNING TEAM	
SECOND REFEREE		LOSING TEAM	

KEYS:

C = Playing Captain
S = Substitution
Sx = Substitution Opponent

—| = Loss Of Rally
R = Replay
RS = Re-Serve

T = Time-Out
Tx = Time-Out Opponent
1,2,3..etc = General Point

P1, P2, P3 = Penalty Point
Px = Penalty Opponent
☐ = Point Scored Off Loss Of Rally
△ = Libero Point

If the receiving team wins the rally, it receives a point which is recorded on the line of the next server's number and a square is drawn around it. Also draw a square around the same point on the team's running score. Draw a triangle around serve order position in which the Libero serves and around all points score by the Libero.

Date:		Location:				Start Time:		Finish Time:	
Home Team:			Visitor Team:			Game No.:		Level:	

Time-Outs		TEAM:				First Serve		Time-Outs		TEAM:	

Running Score

Serve Order	Player No.	Libero # :		Running Score		Serve Order	Player No.	Libero # :

			1 17	1 17			
			2 18	2 18			
I			3 19	3 19	I		
			4 20	4 20			
II			5 21	5 21	II		
			6 22	6 22			
III			7 23	7 23	III		
			8 24	8 24			
IV			9 25	9 25	IV		
			10 26	10 26			
			11 27	11 27			
V			12 28	12 28	V		
			13 29	13 29			
VI			14 30	14 30	VI		
			15 31	15 31			

Substitutions: 1 2 3 4 5 6 7 8 9 10 11 12 13 14 15 16 17 18   16 32   16 32   **Substitutions:** 1 2 3 4 5 6 7 8 9 10 11 12 13 14 15 16 17 18

Comments: **Final Score**   **Comments:**

REFEREE'S VERIFICATION		SCOREKEEPER	
FIRST REFEREE		WINNING TEAM	
SECOND REFEREE		LOSING TEAM	

KEYS:

C = Playing Captain
S = Substitution
Sx = Substitution Opponent

⊣ = Loss Of Rally
R = Replay
RS = Re-Serve

T = Time-Out
Tx = Time-Out Opponent
1,2,3..etc = General Point

P1, P2, P3 = Penalty Point
Px = Penalty Opponent
☐ = Point Scored Off Loss Of Rally
△ = Libero Point

If the receiving team wins the rally, it receives a point which is recorded on the line of the next server's number and a square is drawn around it. Also draw a square around the same point on the team's running score. Draw a triangle around serve order position in which the Libero serves and around all points score by the Libero.

| Date: | | Location: | | | | | | | | | Start Time: | | | Finish Time: | | | |

| Home Team: | | | | Visitor Team: | | | | | | Game No.: | | | Level: | | | |

Time-Outs		TEAM:						First Serve		Time-Outs		TEAM:			

| Serve Order | Player No. | Libero # : | | | | | | Running Score | | Serve Order | Player No. | Libero # : | | | |

Running Score column:
1	17	1	17
2	18	2	18
3	19	3	19
4	20	4	20
5	21	5	21
6	22	6	22
7	23	7	23
8	24	8	24
9	25	9	25
10	26	10	26
11	27	11	27
12	28	12	28
13	29	13	29
14	30	14	30
15	31	15	31
16	32	16	32

Serve Order positions (left team): I, II, III, IV, V, VI
Serve Order positions (right team): I, II, III, IV, V, VI

Substitutions: 1 2 3 4 5 6 7 8 9 10 11 12 13 14 15 16 17 18

Final Score

Substitutions: 1 2 3 4 5 6 7 8 9 10 11 12 13 14 15 16 17 18

Comments:

Comments:

REFEREE'S VERIFICATION		SCOREKEEPER	
FIRST REFEREE		WINNING TEAM	
SECOND REFEREE		LOSING TEAM	

KEYS:

C = Playing Captain
S = Substitution
Sx = Substitution Opponent

━┤ = Loss Of Rally
R = Replay
RS = Re-Serve

T = Time-Out
Tx = Time-Out Opponent
1,2,3..etc = General Point

P1, P2, P3 = Penalty Point
Px = Penalty Opponent
□ = Point Scored Off Loss Of Rally
△ = Libero Point

If the receiving team wins the rally, it receives a point which is recorded on the line of the next server's number and a square is drawn around it. Also draw a square around the same point on the team's running score. Draw a triangle around serve order position in which the Libero serves and around all points score by the Libero.

Date:	Location:		Start Time:	Finish Time:
Home Team:	Visitor Team:		Game No.:	Level:

Time-Outs		TEAM:		First Serve				Time-Outs		TEAM:	

Running Score

Serve Order	Player No.	Libero # :												1	17	1	17	Serve Order	Player No.	Libero # :
														2	18	2	18			
I														3	19	3	19	I		
														4	20	4	20			
II														5	21	5	21	II		
														6	22	6	22			
III														7	23	7	23	III		
														8	24	8	24			
IV														9	25	9	25	IV		
														10	26	10	26			
V														11	27	11	27	V		
														12	28	12	28			
														13	29	13	29			
VI														14	30	14	30	VI		
														15	31	15	31			

Substitutions: 1 2 3 4 5 6 7 8 9 10 11 12 13 14 15 16 17 18	16	32	16	32	Substitutions: 1 2 3 4 5 6 7 8 9 10 11 12 13 14 15 16 17 18
Comments:	**Final Score**		Comments:		

REFEREE'S VERIFICATION		SCOREKEEPER	
FIRST REFEREE		WINNING TEAM	
SECOND REFEREE		LOSING TEAM	

KEYS:

C = Playing Captain
S = Substitution
Sx = Substitution Opponent

—| = Loss Of Rally
R = Replay
RS = Re-Serve

T = Time-Out
Tx = Time-Out Opponent
1,2,3..etc = General Point

P1, P2, P3 = Penalty Point
Px = Penalty Opponent
☐ = Point Scored Off Loss Of Rally
△ = Libero Point

If the receiving team wins the rally, it receives a point which is recorded on the line of the next server's number and a square is drawn around it. Also draw a square around the same point on the team's running score. Draw a triangle around serve order position in which the Libero serves and around all points score by the Libero.

| Date: | | Location: | | | Start Time: | | Finish Time: | |

| Home Team: | | Visitor Team: | | Game No.: | | Level: | |

| Time-Outs | | TEAM: | | First Serve | | Time-Outs | | TEAM: | |

Running Score

| Serve Order | Player No. | Libero # : | | 1 : 17 | 1 : 17 | Serve Order | Player No. | Libero # : |
| | | | 2 : 18 | 2 : 18 | | | |

I — — — — — — — — — — — — — — — — — — — 3 : 19 | 3 : 19 | I

4 : 20 | 4 : 20

II — — — — — — — — — — — — — — — — — — — 5 : 21 | 5 : 21 | II

6 : 22 | 6 : 22

III — — — — — — — — — — — — — — — — — — 7 : 23 | 7 : 23 | III

8 : 24 | 8 : 24

IV — — — — — — — — — — — — — — — — — — 9 : 25 | 9 : 25 | IV

10 : 26 | 10 : 26

V — — — — — — — — — — — — — — — — — — 11 : 27 | 11 : 27 | V

12 : 28 | 12 : 28

13 : 29 | 13 : 29

VI — — — — — — — — — — — — — — — — — — 14 : 30 | 14 : 30 | VI

15 : 31 | 15 : 31

Substitutions: 1 2 3 4 5 6 7 8 9 10 11 12 13 14 15 16 17 18 | 16 : 32 | 16 : 32 | Substitutions: 1 2 3 4 5 6 7 8 9 10 11 12 13 14 15 16 17 18

Comments: | Final Score | Comments:

REFEREE'S VERIFICATION		SCOREKEEPER	
FIRST REFEREE		WINNING TEAM	
SECOND REFEREE		LOSING TEAM	

KEYS:

C = Playing Captain   ⌐| = Loss Of Rally   T = Time-Out   P1, P2, P3 = Penalty Point

S = Substitution   R = Replay   Tx = Time-Out Opponent   Px = Penalty Opponent

Sx = Substitution Opponent   RS = Re-Serve   1,2,3..etc = General Point   ☐ = Point Scored Off Loss Of Rally

△ = Libero Point

If the receiving team wins the rally, it receives a point which is recorded on the line of the next server's number and a square is drawn around it. Also draw a square around the same point on the team's running score. Draw a triangle around serve order position in which the Libero serves and around all points score by the Libero.

Date:		Location:			Start Time:		Finish Time:	
Home Team:			Visitor Team:		Game No.:		Level:	

Time-Outs		TEAM:						First Serve		Time-Outs		TEAM:							

Running Score

Serve Order	Player No.	Libero # :							1 :17 1 :17	Serve Order	Player No.	Libero # :								

I									1 :17 1 :17 2 :18 2 :18	I										
II									3 :19 3 :19 4 :20 4 :20 5 :21 5 :21 6 :22 6 :22	II										
III									7 :23 7 :23 8 :24 8 :24	III										
IV									9 :25 9 :25 10:26 10:26	IV										
V									11:27 11:27 12:28 12:28 13:29 13:29	V										
VI									14:30 14:30 15:31 15:31	VI										

Substitutions: 1 2 3 4 5 6 7 8 9 10 11 12 13 14 15 16 17 18 | 16:32 16:32 | Substitutions: 1 2 3 4 5 6 7 8 9 10 11 12 13 14 15 16 17 18

Comments: | Final Score | Comments:

REFEREE'S VERIFICATION		SCOREKEEPER	
FIRST REFEREE		WINNING TEAM	
SECOND REFEREE		LOSING TEAM	

KEYS:

C = Playing Captain
S = Substitution
Sx = Substitution Opponent

—| = Loss Of Rally
R = Replay
RS = Re-Serve

T = Time-Out
Tx = Time-Out Opponent
1,2,3..etc = General Point

P1, P2, P3 = Penalty Point
Px = Penalty Opponent
☐ = Point Scored Off Loss Of Rally
△ = Libero Point

If the receiving team wins the rally, it receives a point which is recorded on the line of the next server's number and a square is drawn around it. Also draw a square around the same point on the team's running score. Draw a triangle around serve order position in which the Libero serves and around all points score by the Libero.

Date:		Location:						Start Time:		Finish Time:	
Home Team:			Visitor Team:					Game No.:		Level:	

Time-Outs		TEAM:					First Serve		Time-Outs		TEAM:	
							Running Score					

Serve Order	Player No.	Libero # :						Running Score		Serve Order	Player No.	Libero # :							
								1 17	1 17										
I								2 18	2 18	I									
								3 19	3 19										
								4 20	4 20										
II								5 21	5 21	II									
								6 22	6 22										
III								7 23	7 23	III									
								8 24	8 24										
IV								9 25	9 25	IV									
								10 26	10 26										
V								11 27	11 27	V									
								12 28	12 28										
								13 29	13 29										
VI								14 30	14 30	VI									
								15 31	15 31										

Substitutions: 1 2 3 4 5 6 7 8 9 10 11 12 13 14 15 16 17 18

16 32	16 32

Substitutions: 1 2 3 4 5 6 7 8 9 10 11 12 13 14 15 16 17 18

Comments:

Final Score

Comments:

REFEREE'S VERIFICATION		SCOREKEEPER	
FIRST REFEREE		WINNING TEAM	
SECOND REFEREE		LOSING TEAM	

KEYS:

C = Playing Captain
S = Substitution
Sx = Substitution Opponent

—| = Loss Of Rally
R = Replay
RS = Re-Serve

T = Time-Out
Tx = Time-Out Opponent
1,2,3..etc = General Point

P1, P2, P3 = Penalty Point
Px = Penalty Opponent
☐ = Point Scored Off Loss Of Rally
△ = Libero Point

If the receiving team wins the rally, it receives a point which is recorded on the line of the next server's number and a square is drawn around it. Also draw a square around the same point on the team's running score. Draw a triangle around serve order position in which the Libero serves and around all points score by the Libero.

Date:		Location:				Start Time:		Finish Time:	
Home Team:			Visitor Team:			Game No.:		Level:	

Time-Outs		TEAM:			First Serve	Time-Outs		TEAM:	

Serve Order	Player No.	Libero # :				Running Score	Serve Order	Player No.	Libero # :
I						1 17 1 17 / 2 18 2 18	I		
II						3 19 3 19 / 4 20 4 20	II		
III						5 21 5 21 / 6 22 6 22	III		
IV						7 23 7 23 / 8 24 8 24	IV		
V						9 25 9 25 / 10 26 10 26	V		
VI						11 27 11 27 / 12 28 12 28	VI		
						13 29 13 29 / 14 30 14 30			
						15 31 15 31 / 16 32 16 32			

Substitutions: 1 2 3 4 5 6 7 8 9 10 11 12 13 14 15 16 17 18   **Substitutions:** 1 2 3 4 5 6 7 8 9 10 11 12 13 14 15 16 17 18

Comments:

Final Score

Comments:

REFEREE'S VERIFICATION		SCOREKEEPER	
FIRST REFEREE		WINNING TEAM	
SECOND REFEREE		LOSING TEAM	

KEYS:

C = Playing Captain   —| = Loss Of Rally   T = Time-Out   P1, P2, P3 = Penalty Point
S = Substitution   R = Replay   Tx = Time-Out Opponent   Px = Penalty Opponent
Sx = Substitution Opponent   RS = Re-Serve   1,2,3..etc = General Point   ☐ = Point Scored Off Loss Of Rally
△ = Libero Point

If the receiving team wins the rally, it receives a point which is recorded on the line of the next server's number and a square is drawn around it. Also draw a square around the same point on the team's running score. Draw a triangle around serve order position in which the Libero serves and around all points score by the Libero.

Date:	Location:		Start Time:	Finish Time:

Home Team:	Visitor Team:	Game No.:	Level:

Time-Outs		TEAM:		First Serve	Time-Outs		TEAM:	

Running Score

Serve Order	Player No.	Libero # :		1 : 17	1 : 17	Serve Order	Player No.	Libero # :
				2 : 18	2 : 18			
I				3 : 19	3 : 19	I		
				4 : 20	4 : 20			
II				5 : 21	5 : 21	II		
				6 : 22	6 : 22			
III				7 : 23	7 : 23	III		
				8 : 24	8 : 24			
IV				9 : 25	9 : 25	IV		
				10 : 26	10 : 26			
V				11 : 27	11 : 27	V		
				12 : 28	12 : 28			
				13 : 29	13 : 29			
VI				14 : 30	14 : 30	VI		
				15 : 31	15 : 31			

Substitutions: 1 2 3 4 5 6 7 8 9 10 11 12 13 14 15 16 17 18	16 : 32	16 : 32	Substitutions: 1 2 3 4 5 6 7 8 9 10 11 12 13 14 15 16 17 18
Comments:	Final Score		Comments:

REFEREE'S VERIFICATION		SCOREKEEPER	
FIRST REFEREE		WINNING TEAM	
SECOND REFEREE		LOSING TEAM	

KEYS:

C = Playing Captain   ⊣ = Loss Of Rally   T = Time-Out   P1, P2, P3 = Penalty Point

S = Substitution   R = Replay   Tx = Time-Out Opponent   Px = Penalty Opponent

Sx = Substitution Opponent   RS = Re-Serve   1,2,3..etc = General Point   ☐ = Point Scored Off Loss Of Rally

△ = Libero Point

If the receiving team wins the rally, it receives a point which is recorded on the line of the next server's number and a square is drawn around it. Also draw a square around the same point on the team's running score. Draw a triangle around serve order position in which the Libero serves and around all points score by the Libero.

Date:	Location:		Start Time:	Finish Time:
Home Team:	Visitor Team:		Game No.:	Level:

Time-Outs		TEAM:	First Serve	Time-Outs		TEAM:
			Running Score			

Serve Order	Player No.	Libero # :								Running Score	Serve Order	Player No.	Libero # :							
I										1 17 1 17 2 18 2 18	I										
II										3 19 3 19 4 20 4 20	II										
III										5 21 5 21 6 22 6 22	III										
III										7 23 7 23 8 24 8 24	III										
IV										9 25 9 25 10 26 10 26	IV										
V										11 27 11 27 12 28 12 28	V										
VI										13 29 13 29 14 30 14 30 15 31 15 31	VI										

Substitutions: 1 2 3 4 5 6 7 8 9 10 11 12 13 14 15 16 17 18   16 32 16 32   Substitutions: 1 2 3 4 5 6 7 8 9 10 11 12 13 14 15 16 17 18

Comments:	Final Score	Comments:

REFEREE'S VERIFICATION		SCOREKEEPER	
FIRST REFEREE		WINNING TEAM	
SECOND REFEREE		LOSING TEAM	

KEYS:

C = Playing Captain
S = Substitution
Sx = Substitution Opponent

—| = Loss Of Rally
R = Replay
RS = Re-Serve

T = Time-Out
Tx = Time-Out Opponent
1,2,3..etc = General Point

P1, P2, P3 = Penalty Point
Px = Penalty Opponent
☐ = Point Scored Off Loss Of Rally
△ = Libero Point

If the receiving team wins the rally, it receives a point which is recorded on the line of the next server's number and a square is drawn around it. Also draw a square around the same point on the team's running score. Draw a triangle around serve order position in which the Libero serves and around all points score by the Libero.

Date:	Location:		Start Time:	Finish Time:

Home Team:	Visitor Team:	Game No.:	Level:

Time-Outs		TEAM:	First Serve	Time-Outs		TEAM:

			Running Score			

Serve Order	Player No.	Libero # :		Serve Order	Player No.	Libero # :

Running Score (left)	Running Score (right)
1 17	1 17
2 18	2 18
3 19	3 19
4 20	4 20
5 21	5 21
6 22	6 22
7 23	7 23
8 24	8 24
9 25	9 25
10 26	10 26
11 27	11 27
12 28	12 28
13 29	13 29
14 30	14 30
15 31	15 31
16 32	16 32

Serve Order positions: I, II, III, IV, V, VI

Substitutions: 1 2 3 4 5 6 7 8 9 10 11 12 13 14 15 16 17 18

Substitutions: 1 2 3 4 5 6 7 8 9 10 11 12 13 14 15 16 17 18

Comments:

Final Score

Comments:

REFEREE'S VERIFICATION		SCOREKEEPER	
FIRST REFEREE		WINNING TEAM	
SECOND REFEREE		LOSING TEAM	

KEYS:

C = Playing Captain
S = Substitution
Sx = Substitution Opponent

—| = Loss Of Rally
R = Replay
RS = Re-Serve

T = Time-Out
Tx = Time-Out Opponent
1,2,3..etc = General Point

P1, P2, P3 = Penalty Point
Px = Penalty Opponent
☐ = Point Scored Off Loss Of Rally
△ = Libero Point

If the receiving team wins the rally, it receives a point which is recorded on the line of the next server's number and a square is drawn around it. Also draw a square around the same point on the team's running score. Draw a triangle around serve order position in which the Libero serves and around all points score by the Libero.

Date:		Location:						Start Time:		Finish Time:	
Home Team:			Visitor Team:					Game No.:		Level:	

Time-Outs		TEAM:		First Serve		Time-Outs		TEAM:	
				Running Score					

Serve Order	Player No.	Libero # :								1 17	1 17	Serve Order	Player No.	Libero # :							
										2 18	2 18										
I		- - - - -								3 19	3 19	I		- - - - -							
										4 20	4 20										
II		- - - - -								5 21	5 21	II		- - - - -							
										6 22	6 22										
III		- - - - -								7 23	7 23	III		- - - - -							
										8 24	8 24										
IV		- - - - -								9 25	9 25	IV		- - - - -							
										10 26	10 26										
V		- - - - -								11 27	11 27	V		- - - - -							
										12 28	12 28										
VI		- - - - -								13 29	13 29	VI		- - - - -							
										14 30	14 30										
										15 31	15 31										

Substitutions: 1 2 3 4 5 6 7 8 9 10 11 12 13 14 15 16 17 18 | 16 32 | 16 32 | **Substitutions:** 1 2 3 4 5 6 7 8 9 10 11 12 13 14 15 16 17 18

Comments: | Final Score | **Comments:**

REFEREE'S VERIFICATION		SCOREKEEPER	
FIRST REFEREE		WINNING TEAM	
SECOND REFEREE		LOSING TEAM	

KEYS:

C = Playing Captain   ▬❙ = Loss Of Rally   T = Time-Out   P1, P2, P3 = Penalty Point

S = Substitution   R = Replay   Tx = Time-Out Opponent   Px = Penalty Opponent

Sx = Substitution Opponent   RS = Re-Serve   1,2,3..etc = General Point   ☐ = Point Scored Off Loss Of Rally

△ = Libero Point

If the receiving team wins the rally, it receives a point which is recorded on the line of the next server's number and a square is drawn around it. Also draw a square around the same point on the team's running score. Draw a triangle around serve order position in which the Libero serves and around all points score by the Libero.

Date:	Location:		Start Time:	Finish Time:
Home Team:	Visitor Team:		Game No.:	Level:

Time-Outs		TEAM:	First Serve	Time-Outs		TEAM:
			Running Score			

Serve Order	Player No.	Libero # :										Running Score	Serve Order	Player No.	Libero # :									
I												1 17 1 17 / 2 18 2 18	I												
II												3 19 3 19 / 4 20 4 20	II												
III												5 21 5 21 / 6 22 6 22	III												
IV												7 23 7 23 / 8 24 8 24	IV												
V												9 25 9 25 / 10 26 10 26	V												
VI												11 27 11 27 / 12 28 12 28 / 13 29 13 29 / 14 30 14 30 / 15 31 15 31	VI												

Substitutions: 1 2 3 4 5 6 7 8 9 10 11 12 13 14 15 16 17 18	16 32 16 32	Substitutions: 1 2 3 4 5 6 7 8 9 10 11 12 13 14 15 16 17 18
Comments:	Final Score	Comments:

REFEREE'S VERIFICATION		SCOREKEEPER	
FIRST REFEREE		WINNING TEAM	
SECOND REFEREE		LOSING TEAM	

KEYS:

C = Playing Captain
S = Substitution
Sx = Substitution Opponent

⊣ = Loss Of Rally
R = Replay
RS = Re-Serve

T = Time-Out
Tx = Time-Out Opponent
1,2,3..etc = General Point

P1, P2, P3 = Penalty Point
Px = Penalty Opponent
☐ = Point Scored Off Loss Of Rally
△ = Libero Point

If the receiving team wins the rally, it receives a point which is recorded on the line of the next server's number and a square is drawn around it. Also draw a square around the same point on the team's running score. Draw a triangle around serve order position in which the Libero serves and around all points score by the Libero.

Date:	Location:		Start Time:	Finish Time:
Home Team:		Visitor Team:	Game No.:	Level:

Time-Outs	TEAM:	First Serve	Time-Outs	TEAM:

Running Score

Serve Order	Player No.	Libero # :											1 17 1 17	Serve Order	Player No.	Libero # :

Running Score column values:
1 17 | 1 17
2 18 | 2 18
3 19 | 3 19
4 20 | 4 20
5 21 | 5 21
6 22 | 6 22
7 23 | 7 23
8 24 | 8 24
9 25 | 9 25
10 26 | 10 26
11 27 | 11 27
12 28 | 12 28
13 29 | 13 29
14 30 | 14 30
15 31 | 15 31
16 32 | 16 32

Serve Order left: I, II, III, IV, V, VI
Serve Order right: I, II, III, IV, V, VI

Substitutions: 1 2 3 4 5 6 7 8 9 10 11 12 13 14 15 16 17 18   Final Score   Substitutions: 1 2 3 4 5 6 7 8 9 10 11 12 13 14 15 16 17 18

Comments: Comments:

REFEREE'S VERIFICATION		SCOREKEEPER	
FIRST REFEREE		WINNING TEAM	
SECOND REFEREE		LOSING TEAM	

KEYS:

C = Playing Captain
S = Substitution
Sx = Substitution Opponent

—| = Loss Of Rally
R = Replay
RS = Re-Serve

T = Time-Out
Tx = Time-Out Opponent
1,2,3..etc = General Point

P1, P2, P3 = Penalty Point
Px = Penalty Opponent
☐ = Point Scored Off Loss Of Rally
△ = Libero Point

If the receiving team wins the rally, it receives a point which is recorded on the line of the next server's number and a square is drawn around it. Also draw a square around the same point on the team's running score. Draw a triangle around serve order position in which the Libero serves and around all points score by the Libero.

Date:	Location:		Start Time:	Finish Time:
Home Team:	Visitor Team:		Game No.:	Level:

Time-Outs		TEAM:	First Serve	Time-Outs		TEAM:

Running Score

Serve Order	Player No.	Libero # :							1 17 1 17	Serve Order	Player No.	Libero # :
									2 18 2 18			
I									3 19 3 19	I		
									4 20 4 20			
II									5 21 5 21	II		
									6 22 6 22			
III									7 23 7 23	III		
									8 24 8 24			
IV									9 25 9 25	IV		
									10 26 10 26			
V									11 27 11 27	V		
									12 28 12 28			
									13 29 13 29			
VI									14 30 14 30	VI		
									15 31 15 31			

Substitutions: 1 2 3 4 5 6 7 8 9 10 11 12 13 14 15 16 17 18 | 16 32 16 32 | **Substitutions:** 1 2 3 4 5 6 7 8 9 10 11 12 13 14 15 16 17 18

Comments: | **Final Score** | **Comments:**

REFEREE'S VERIFICATION		SCOREKEEPER	
FIRST REFEREE		WINNING TEAM	
SECOND REFEREE		LOSING TEAM	

KEYS:

C = Playing Captain
S = Substitution
Sx = Substitution Opponent

—| = Loss Of Rally
R = Replay
RS = Re-Serve

T = Time-Out
Tx = Time-Out Opponent
1,2,3..etc = General Point

P1, P2, P3 = Penalty Point
Px = Penalty Opponent
☐ = Point Scored Off Loss Of Rally
△ = Libero Point

If the receiving team wins the rally, it receives a point which is recorded on the line of the next server's number and a square is drawn around it. Also draw a square around the same point on the team's running score. Draw a triangle around serve order position in which the Libero serves and around all points score by the Libero.

Date:	Location:	Start Time:	Finish Time:
Home Team:	Visitor Team:	Game No.:	Level:

Time-Outs		TEAM:										
Serve Order	Player No.	Libero # :										
I												
II												
III												
IV												
V												
VI												

Substitutions: 1 2 3 4 5 6 7 8 9 10 11 12 13 14 15 16 17 18

Comments:

First Serve			
Running Score			
1	17	1	17
2	18	2	18
3	19	3	19
4	20	4	20
5	21	5	21
6	22	6	22
7	23	7	23
8	24	8	24
9	25	9	25
10	26	10	26
11	27	11	27
12	28	12	28
13	29	13	29
14	30	14	30
15	31	15	31
16	32	16	32
Final Score			

Time-Outs		TEAM:										
Serve Order	Player No.	Libero # :										
I												
II												
III												
IV												
V												
VI												

Substitutions: 1 2 3 4 5 6 7 8 9 10 11 12 13 14 15 16 17 18

Comments:

REFEREE'S VERIFICATION		SCOREKEEPER	
FIRST REFEREE		WINNING TEAM	
SECOND REFEREE		LOSING TEAM	

KEYS:

C = Playing Captain
S = Substitution
Sx = Substitution Opponent

—| = Loss Of Rally
R = Replay
RS = Re-Serve

T = Time-Out
Tx = Time-Out Opponent
1,2,3..etc = General Point

P1, P2, P3 = Penalty Point
Px = Penalty Opponent
□ = Point Scored Off Loss Of Rally
△ = Libero Point

If the receiving team wins the rally, it receives a point which is recorded on the line of the next server's number and a square is drawn around it. Also draw a square around the same point on the team's running score. Draw a triangle around serve order position in which the Libero serves and around all points score by the Libero.

Date:	Location:		Start Time:	Finish Time:
Home Team:	Visitor Team:		Game No.:	Level:

Time-Outs	TEAM:		First Serve	Time-Outs	TEAM:

Running Score

Serve Order	Player No.	Libero # :		1	17	1	17	Serve Order	Player No.	Libero # :
				2	18	2	18			
I				3	19	3	19	I		
				4	20	4	20			
II				5	21	5	21	II		
				6	22	6	22			
III				7	23	7	23	III		
				8	24	8	24			
IV				9	25	9	25	IV		
				10	26	10	26			
V				11	27	11	27	V		
				12	28	12	28			
				13	29	13	29			
VI				14	30	14	30	VI		
				15	31	15	31			

Substitutions: 1 2 3 4 5 6 7 8 9 10 11 12 13 14 15 16 17 18 | 16 32 | 16 32 | Substitutions: 1 2 3 4 5 6 7 8 9 10 11 12 13 14 15 16 17 18

Comments: | Final Score | Comments:

REFEREE'S VERIFICATION		SCOREKEEPER	
FIRST REFEREE		WINNING TEAM	
SECOND REFEREE		LOSING TEAM	

KEYS:

C = Playing Captain
S = Substitution
Sx = Substitution Opponent

—| = Loss Of Rally
R = Replay
RS = Re-Serve

T = Time-Out
Tx = Time-Out Opponent
1,2,3..etc = General Point

P1, P2, P3 = Penalty Point
Px = Penalty Opponent
□ = Point Scored Off Loss Of Rally
△ = Libero Point

If the receiving team wins the rally, it receives a point which is recorded on the line of the next server's number and a square is drawn around it. Also draw a square around the same point on the team's running score. Draw a triangle around serve order position in which the Libero serves and around all points score by the Libero.

Date:	Location:		Start Time:	Finish Time:
Home Team:	Visitor Team:		Game No.:	Level:

Time-Outs		TEAM:	First Serve	Time-Outs		TEAM:
			Running Score			

Serve Order	Player No.	Libero # :	1 17 1 17	Serve Order	Player No.	Libero # :
			2 18 2 18			
I			3 19 3 19	I		
			4 20 4 20			
II			5 21 5 21	II		
			6 22 6 22			
III			7 23 7 23	III		
			8 24 8 24			
IV			9 25 9 25	IV		
			10 26 10 26			
V			11 27 11 27	V		
			12 28 12 28			
VI			13 29 13 29	VI		
			14 30 14 30			
			15 31 15 31			

Substitutions: 1 2 3 4 5 6 7 8 9 10 11 12 13 14 15 16 17 18 | 16 32 16 32 | **Substitutions:** 1 2 3 4 5 6 7 8 9 10 11 12 13 14 15 16 17 18

Comments: | Final Score | **Comments:**

REFEREE'S VERIFICATION		SCOREKEEPER	
FIRST REFEREE		WINNING TEAM	
SECOND REFEREE		LOSING TEAM	

KEYS:

C = Playing Captain

S = Substitution

Sx = Substitution Opponent

⊣ = Loss Of Rally

R = Replay

RS = Re-Serve

T = Time-Out

Tx = Time-Out Opponent

1,2,3..etc = General Point

P1, P2, P3 = Penalty Point

Px = Penalty Opponent

☐ = Point Scored Off Loss Of Rally

△ = Libero Point

If the receiving team wins the rally, it receives a point which is recorded on the line of the next server's number and a square is drawn around it. Also draw a square around the same point on the team's running score. Draw a triangle around serve order position in which the Libero serves and around all points score by the Libero.

Date:		Location:							Start Time:		Finish Time:	
Home Team:			Visitor Team:						Game No.:		Level:	

| Time-Outs | | TEAM: | | | | | | | First Serve | | Time-Outs | | TEAM: | | | | | | |

									Running Score										
Serve Order	Player No.	Libero # :							1 ¦ 17	1 ¦ 17	Serve Order	Player No.	Libero # :						
									2 ¦ 18	2 ¦ 18									
I									3 ¦ 19	3 ¦ 19	I								
									4 ¦ 20	4 ¦ 20									
II									5 ¦ 21	5 ¦ 21	II								
									6 ¦ 22	6 ¦ 22									
III									7 ¦ 23	7 ¦ 23	III								
									8 ¦ 24	8 ¦ 24									
IV									9 ¦ 25	9 ¦ 25	IV								
									10 ¦ 26	10 ¦ 26									
V									11 ¦ 27	11 ¦ 27	V								
									12 ¦ 28	12 ¦ 28									
									13 ¦ 29	13 ¦ 29									
VI									14 ¦ 30	14 ¦ 30	VI								
									15 ¦ 31	15 ¦ 31									

Substitutions: 1 2 3 4 5 6 7 8 9 10 11 12 13 14 15 16 17 18	16 ¦ 32	16 ¦ 32	Substitutions: 1 2 3 4 5 6 7 8 9 10 11 12 13 14 15 16 17 18
Comments:	Final Score		Comments:

REFEREE'S VERIFICATION		SCOREKEEPER	
FIRST REFEREE		WINNING TEAM	
SECOND REFEREE		LOSING TEAM	

KEYS:

C = Playing Captain

S = Substitution

Sx = Substitution Opponent

—| = Loss Of Rally

R = Replay

RS = Re-Serve

T = Time-Out

Tx = Time-Out Opponent

1,2,3..etc = General Point

P1, P2, P3 = Penalty Point

Px = Penalty Opponent

☐ = Point Scored Off Loss Of Rally

△ = Libero Point

If the receiving team wins the rally, it receives a point which is recorded on the line of the next server's number and a square is drawn around it. Also draw a square around the same point on the team's running score. Draw a triangle around serve order position in which the Libero serves and around all points score by the Libero.

Date:	Location:		Start Time:	Finish Time:
Home Team:	Visitor Team:		Game No.:	Level:

Time-Outs	TEAM:				First Serve	Time-Outs	TEAM:		
					Running Score				

Serve Order	Player No.	Libero # :			Running Score	Serve Order	Player No.	Libero # :	
I				1 17 1 17		I			
				2 18 2 18					
				3 19 3 19					
				4 20 4 20					
II				5 21 5 21		II			
				6 22 6 22					
III				7 23 7 23		III			
				8 24 8 24					
IV				9 25 9 25		IV			
				10 26 10 26					
V				11 27 11 27		V			
				12 28 12 28					
				13 29 13 29					
VI				14 30 14 30		VI			
				15 31 15 31					

Substitutions: 1 2 3 4 5 6 7 8 9 10 11 12 13 14 15 16 17 18 | 16 32 16 32 | Substitutions: 1 2 3 4 5 6 7 8 9 10 11 12 13 14 15 16 17 18

Comments: | Final Score | Comments:

REFEREE'S VERIFICATION		SCOREKEEPER	
FIRST REFEREE		WINNING TEAM	
SECOND REFEREE		LOSING TEAM	

KEYS:

C = Playing Captain   —| = Loss Of Rally   T = Time-Out   P1, P2, P3 = Penalty Point

S = Substitution   R = Replay   Tx = Time-Out Opponent   Px = Penalty Opponent

Sx = Substitution Opponent   RS = Re-Serve   1,2,3..etc = General Point   ☐ = Point Scored Off Loss Of Rally

△ = Libero Point

If the receiving team wins the rally, it receives a point which is recorded on the line of the next server's number and a square is drawn around it. Also draw a square around the same point on the team's running score. Draw a triangle around serve order position in which the Libero serves and around all points score by the Libero.

Date:		Location:								Start Time:			Finish Time:	
Home Team:				Visitor Team:						Game No.:			Level:	

Time-Outs		TEAM:							First Serve			Time-Outs		TEAM:

Running Score

Serve Order	Player No.	Libero # :							1	17	1	17	Serve Order	Player No.	Libero # :
									2	18	2	18			
I									3	19	3	19	I		
									4	20	4	20			
II									5	21	5	21	II		
									6	22	6	22			
III									7	23	7	23	III		
									8	24	8	24			
IV									9	25	9	25	IV		
									10	26	10	26			
V									11	27	11	27	V		
									12	28	12	28			
									13	29	13	29			
VI									14	30	14	30	VI		
									15	31	15	31			

Substitutions: 1 2 3 4 5 6 7 8 9 10 11 12 13 14 15 16 17 18 | 16 32 16 32 | Substitutions: 1 2 3 4 5 6 7 8 9 10 11 12 13 14 15 16 17 18

Comments: | Final Score | Comments:

REFEREE'S VERIFICATION		SCOREKEEPER	
FIRST REFEREE		WINNING TEAM	
SECOND REFEREE		LOSING TEAM	

KEYS:

C = Playing Captain   —| = Loss Of Rally   T = Time-Out   P1, P2, P3 = Penalty Point

S = Substitution   R = Replay   Tx = Time-Out Opponent   Px = Penalty Opponent

Sx = Substitution Opponent   RS = Re-Serve   1,2,3..etc = General Point   ☐ = Point Scored Off Loss Of Rally

△ = Libero Point

If the receiving team wins the rally, it receives a point which is recorded on the line of the next server's number and a square is drawn around it. Also draw a square around the same point on the team's running score. Draw a triangle around serve order position in which the Libero serves and around all points score by the Libero.

| Date: | | Location: | | | | Start Time: | | Finish Time: | |

| Home Team: | | Visitor Team: | | | Game No.: | | Level: | |

| **Time-Outs** | | TEAM: | | | | | | | **First Serve** | **Time-Outs** | | TEAM: | | | | | | |

<table>
<tr><th colspan="2">Time-Outs</th><th>TEAM:</th><th></th><th></th><th></th><th></th><th></th><th></th><th>First Serve</th><th colspan="2">Time-Outs</th><th>TEAM:</th><th></th><th></th><th></th><th></th><th></th><th></th></tr>
<tr><td colspan="2"></td><td colspan="7"></td><td>Running Score</td><td colspan="2"></td><td colspan="7"></td></tr>
<tr><td>Serve Order</td><td>Player No.</td><td colspan="7">Libero # :</td><td>1 ¦ 17 1 ¦ 17
2 ¦ 18 2 ¦ 18</td><td>Serve Order</td><td>Player No.</td><td colspan="7">Libero # :</td></tr>
<tr><td>I</td><td></td><td></td><td></td><td></td><td></td><td></td><td></td><td></td><td>3 ¦ 19 3 ¦ 19
4 ¦ 20 4 ¦ 20</td><td>I</td><td></td><td></td><td></td><td></td><td></td><td></td><td></td><td></td></tr>
<tr><td>II</td><td></td><td></td><td></td><td></td><td></td><td></td><td></td><td></td><td>5 ¦ 21 5 ¦ 21
6 ¦ 22 6 ¦ 22</td><td>II</td><td></td><td></td><td></td><td></td><td></td><td></td><td></td><td></td></tr>
<tr><td>III</td><td></td><td></td><td></td><td></td><td></td><td></td><td></td><td></td><td>7 ¦ 23 7 ¦ 23
8 ¦ 24 8 ¦ 24</td><td>III</td><td></td><td></td><td></td><td></td><td></td><td></td><td></td><td></td></tr>
<tr><td>IV</td><td></td><td></td><td></td><td></td><td></td><td></td><td></td><td></td><td>9 ¦ 25 9 ¦ 25
10 ¦ 26 10 ¦ 26</td><td>IV</td><td></td><td></td><td></td><td></td><td></td><td></td><td></td><td></td></tr>
<tr><td>V</td><td></td><td></td><td></td><td></td><td></td><td></td><td></td><td></td><td>11 ¦ 27 11 ¦ 27
12 ¦ 28 12 ¦ 28</td><td>V</td><td></td><td></td><td></td><td></td><td></td><td></td><td></td><td></td></tr>
<tr><td>VI</td><td></td><td></td><td></td><td></td><td></td><td></td><td></td><td></td><td>13 ¦ 29 13 ¦ 29
14 ¦ 30 14 ¦ 30
15 ¦ 31 15 ¦ 31</td><td>VI</td><td></td><td></td><td></td><td></td><td></td><td></td><td></td><td></td></tr>
</table>

Substitutions: 1 2 3 4 5 6 7 8 9 10 11 12 13 14 15 16 17 18 | 16 ¦ 32 16 ¦ 32 | Substitutions: 1 2 3 4 5 6 7 8 9 10 11 12 13 14 15 16 17 18

Comments: | Final Score | Comments:

REFEREE'S VERIFICATION		SCOREKEEPER	
FIRST REFEREE		WINNING TEAM	
SECOND REFEREE		LOSING TEAM	

KEYS:

C = Playing Captain   ▬| = Loss Of Rally   T = Time-Out   P1, P2, P3 = Penalty Point

S = Substitution   R = Replay   Tx = Time-Out Opponent   Px = Penalty Opponent

Sx = Substitution Opponent   RS = Re-Serve   1,2,3..etc = General Point   ☐ = Point Scored Off Loss Of Rally

△ = Libero Point

If the receiving team wins the rally, it receives a point which is recorded on the line of the next server's number and a square is drawn around it. Also draw a square around the same point on the team's running score. Draw a triangle around serve order position in which the Libero serves and around all points score by the Libero.

Date:	Location:		Start Time:	Finish Time:
Home Team:	Visitor Team:		Game No.:	Level:

Time-Outs		TEAM:								First Serve		Time-Outs		TEAM:							
										Running Score												
Serve Order	Player No.	Libero # :								1 17 1 17		Serve Order	Player No.	Libero # :								
										2 18 2 18												
I										3 19 3 19		I										
										4 20 4 20												
II										5 21 5 21		II										
										6 22 6 22												
III										7 23 7 23		III										
										8 24 8 24												
IV										9 25 9 25		IV										
										10 26 10 26												
V										11 27 11 27		V										
										12 28 12 28												
										13 29 13 29												
VI										14 30 14 30		VI										
										15 31 15 31												

Substitutions:1 2 3 4 5 6 7 8 9 10 11 12 13 14 15 16 17 18	16 32 16 32	Substitutions:1 2 3 4 5 6 7 8 9 10 11 12 13 14 15 16 17 18
Comments:	Final Score	Comments:

REFEREE'S VERIFICATION		SCOREKEEPER	
FIRST REFEREE		WINNING TEAM	
SECOND REFEREE		LOSING TEAM	

KEYS:

C = Playing Captain   —| = Loss Of Rally   T = Time-Out   P1, P2, P3 = Penalty Point

S = Substitution   R = Replay   Tx = Time-Out Opponent   Px = Penalty Opponent

Sx = Substitution Opponent   RS = Re-Serve   1,2,3..etc = General Point   □ = Point Scored Off Loss Of Rally

△ = Libero Point

If the receiving team wins the rally, it receives a point which is recorded on the line of the next server's number and a square is drawn around it. Also draw a square around the same point on the team's running score. Draw a triangle around serve order position in which the Libero serves and around all points score by the Libero.

Date:	Location:		Start Time:	Finish Time:
Home Team:	Visitor Team:		Game No.:	Level:

Time-Outs	TEAM:		First Serve	Time-Outs	TEAM:

			Running Score			

Serve Order	Player No.	Libero # :	1 : 17 1 : 17	Serve Order	Player No.	Libero # :
			2 : 18 2 : 18			
I			3 : 19 3 : 19	I		
			4 : 20 4 : 20			
II			5 : 21 5 : 21	II		
			6 : 22 6 : 22			
III			7 : 23 7 : 23	III		
			8 : 24 8 : 24			
IV			9 : 25 9 : 25	IV		
			10 : 26 10 : 26			
V			11 : 27 11 : 27	V		
			12 : 28 12 : 28			
			13 : 29 13 : 29			
VI			14 : 30 14 : 30	VI		
			15 : 31 15 : 31			

Substitutions: 1 2 3 4 5 6 7 8 9 10 11 12 13 14 15 16 17 18	16 : 32 16 : 32	Substitutions: 1 2 3 4 5 6 7 8 9 10 11 12 13 14 15 16 17 18
Comments:	Final Score	Comments:

REFEREE'S VERIFICATION		SCOREKEEPER	
FIRST REFEREE		WINNING TEAM	
SECOND REFEREE		LOSING TEAM	

KEYS:

C = Playing Captain

S = Substitution

Sx = Substitution Opponent

▬| = Loss Of Rally

R = Replay

RS = Re-Serve

T = Time-Out

Tx = Time-Out Opponent

1,2,3..etc = General Point

P1, P2, P3 = Penalty Point

Px = Penalty Opponent

☐ = Point Scored Off Loss Of Rally

△ = Libero Point

If the receiving team wins the rally, it receives a point which is recorded on the line of the next server's number and a square is drawn around it. Also draw a square around the same point on the team's running score. Draw a triangle around serve order position in which the Libero serves and around all points score by the Libero.

Date:		Location:					Start Time:		Finish Time:	
Home Team:			Visitor Team:				Game No.:		Level:	

Time-Outs		TEAM:										First Serve		Time-Outs		TEAM:								

Running Score

Serve Order	Player No.	Libero # :										Running Score		Serve Order	Player No.	Libero # :								
												1 17 | 1 17												
												2 18 | 2 18												
I												3 19 | 3 19		I										
												4 20 | 4 20												
II												5 21 | 5 21		II										
												6 22 | 6 22												
III												7 23 | 7 23		III										
												8 24 | 8 24												
IV												9 25 | 9 25		IV										
												10 26 | 10 26												
V												11 27 | 11 27		V										
												12 28 | 12 28												
												13 29 | 13 29												
VI												14 30 | 14 30		VI										
												15 31 | 15 31												

Substitutions: 1 2 3 4 5 6 7 8 9 10 11 12 13 14 15 16 17 18 | 16 32 \| 16 32 | Substitutions: 1 2 3 4 5 6 7 8 9 10 11 12 13 14 15 16 17 18

Comments: | **Final Score** | Comments:

REFEREE'S VERIFICATION		SCOREKEEPER	
FIRST REFEREE		WINNING TEAM	
SECOND REFEREE		LOSING TEAM	

KEYS:

C = Playing Captain   ━| = Loss Of Rally   T = Time-Out   P1, P2, P3 = Penalty Point

S = Substitution   R = Replay   Tx = Time-Out Opponent   Px = Penalty Opponent

Sx = Substitution Opponent   RS = Re-Serve   1,2,3..etc = General Point   ☐ = Point Scored Off Loss Of Rally

△ = Libero Point

If the receiving team wins the rally, it receives a point which is recorded on the line of the next server's number and a square is drawn around it. Also draw a square around the same point on the team's running score. Draw a triangle around serve order position in which the Libero serves and around all points score by the Libero.

Date:		Location:					Start Time:		Finish Time:	
Home Team:			Visitor Team:				Game No.:		Level:	

Time-Outs		TEAM:							First Serve		Time-Outs		TEAM:					

Running Score

Serve Order	Player No.	Libero # :									1 17	1 17	Serve Order	Player No.	Libero # :
											2 18	2 18			
I											3 19	3 19	I		
											4 20	4 20			
II											5 21	5 21	II		
											6 22	6 22			
III											7 23	7 23	III		
											8 24	8 24			
IV											9 25	9 25	IV		
											10 26	10 26			
V											11 27	11 27	V		
											12 28	12 28			
VI											13 29	13 29	VI		
											14 30	14 30			
											15 31	15 31			

Substitutions: 1 2 3 4 5 6 7 8 9 10 11 12 13 14 15 16 17 18 | 16 32 | 16 32 | Substitutions: 1 2 3 4 5 6 7 8 9 10 11 12 13 14 15 16 17 18

Comments:

Final Score

Comments:

REFEREE'S VERIFICATION		SCOREKEEPER	
FIRST REFEREE		WINNING TEAM	
SECOND REFEREE		LOSING TEAM	

KEYS:

C = Playing Captain   ▬| = Loss Of Rally   T = Time-Out   P1, P2, P3 = Penalty Point

S = Substitution   R = Replay   Tx = Time-Out Opponent   Px = Penalty Opponent

Sx = Substitution Opponent   RS = Re-Serve   1,2,3..etc = General Point   ☐ = Point Scored Off Loss Of Rally

△ = Libero Point

If the receiving team wins the rally, it receives a point which is recorded on the line of the next server's number and a square is drawn around it. Also draw a square around the same point on the team's running score. Draw a triangle around serve order position in which the Libero serves and around all points score by the Libero.

Date:	Location:		Start Time:	Finish Time:
Home Team:	Visitor Team:		Game No.:	Level:

Time-Outs		TEAM:		First Serve	Time-Outs		TEAM:	

Running Score

Serve Order	Player No.	Libero # :		1 17	1 17	Serve Order	Player No.	Libero # :
				2 18	2 18			
I				3 19	3 19	I		
				4 20	4 20			
II				5 21	5 21	II		
				6 22	6 22			
III				7 23	7 23	III		
				8 24	8 24			
IV				9 25	9 25	IV		
				10 26	10 26			
V				11 27	11 27	V		
				12 28	12 28			
				13 29	13 29			
VI				14 30	14 30	VI		
				15 31	15 31			

Substitutions: 1 2 3 4 5 6 7 8 9 10 11 12 13 14 15 16 17 18	16 32	16 32	Substitutions: 1 2 3 4 5 6 7 8 9 10 11 12 13 14 15 16 17 18
Comments:	Final Score		Comments:

REFEREE'S VERIFICATION		SCOREKEEPER	
FIRST REFEREE		WINNING TEAM	
SECOND REFEREE		LOSING TEAM	

KEYS:

C = Playing Captain
S = Substitution
Sx = Substitution Opponent

—| = Loss Of Rally
R = Replay
RS = Re-Serve

T = Time-Out
Tx = Time-Out Opponent
1,2,3..etc = General Point

P1, P2, P3 = Penalty Point
Px = Penalty Opponent
□ = Point Scored Off Loss Of Rally
△ = Libero Point

If the receiving team wins the rally, it receives a point which is recorded on the line of the next server's number and a square is drawn around it. Also draw a square around the same point on the team's running score. Draw a triangle around serve order position in which the Libero serves and around all points score by the Libero.

Date:		Location:				Start Time:		Finish Time:	
Home Team:			Visitor Team:			Game No.:		Level:	

Time-Outs		TEAM:						First Serve				Time-Outs		TEAM:			

Running Score

Serve Order	Player No.	Libero # :							1	17	1	17	Serve Order	Player No.	Libero # :			
									2	18	2	18						
I									3	19	3	19	I					
									4	20	4	20						
II									5	21	5	21	II					
									6	22	6	22						
III									7	23	7	23	III					
									8	24	8	24						
IV									9	25	9	25	IV					
									10	26	10	26						
V									11	27	11	27	V					
									12	28	12	28						
									13	29	13	29						
VI									14	30	14	30	VI					
									15	31	15	31						

Substitutions: 1 2 3 4 5 6 7 8 9 10 11 12 13 14 15 16 17 18	16 32 16 32	Substitutions: 1 2 3 4 5 6 7 8 9 10 11 12 13 14 15 16 17 18
Comments:	Final Score	Comments:

REFEREE'S VERIFICATION		SCOREKEEPER	
FIRST REFEREE		WINNING TEAM	
SECOND REFEREE		LOSING TEAM	

KEYS:

C = Playing Captain
S = Substitution
Sx = Substitution Opponent

▬| = Loss Of Rally
R = Replay
RS = Re-Serve

T = Time-Out
Tx = Time-Out Opponent
1,2,3..etc = General Point

P1, P2, P3 = Penalty Point
Px = Penalty Opponent
☐ = Point Scored Off Loss Of Rally
△ = Libero Point

If the receiving team wins the rally, it receives a point which is recorded on the line of the next server's number and a square is drawn around it. Also draw a square around the same point on the team's running score. Draw a triangle around serve order position in which the Libero serves and around all points score by the Libero.

| Date: | | Location: | | | | Start Time: | | Finish Time: | |

| Home Team: | | Visitor Team: | | | Game No.: | | Level: | |

| Time-Outs | | TEAM: | | | First Serve | Time-Outs | | TEAM: | |

Running Score

| Serve Order | Player No. | Libero # : | | | Running Score | Serve Order | Player No. | Libero # : | |

			First Serve Running Score				

Running Score columns:
1 ¦ 17 | 1 ¦ 17
2 ¦ 18 | 2 ¦ 18
3 ¦ 19 | 3 ¦ 19
4 ¦ 20 | 4 ¦ 20
5 ¦ 21 | 5 ¦ 21
6 ¦ 22 | 6 ¦ 22
7 ¦ 23 | 7 ¦ 23
8 ¦ 24 | 8 ¦ 24
9 ¦ 25 | 9 ¦ 25
10 ¦ 26 | 10 ¦ 26
11 ¦ 27 | 11 ¦ 27
12 ¦ 28 | 12 ¦ 28
13 ¦ 29 | 13 ¦ 29
14 ¦ 30 | 14 ¦ 30
15 ¦ 31 | 15 ¦ 31
16 ¦ 32 | 16 ¦ 32

Serve Order rows (left and right): I, II, III, IV, V, VI

Substitutions: 1 2 3 4 5 6 7 8 9 10 11 12 13 14 15 16 17 18

Final Score

Substitutions: 1 2 3 4 5 6 7 8 9 10 11 12 13 14 15 16 17 18

Comments:

Comments:

REFEREE'S VERIFICATION		SCOREKEEPER	
FIRST REFEREE		WINNING TEAM	
SECOND REFEREE		LOSING TEAM	

KEYS:

C = Playing Captain
S = Substitution
Sx = Substitution Opponent

—| = Loss Of Rally
R = Replay
RS = Re-Serve

T = Time-Out
Tx = Time-Out Opponent
1,2,3..etc = General Point

P1, P2, P3 = Penalty Point
Px = Penalty Opponent
☐ = Point Scored Off Loss Of Rally
△ = Libero Point

If the receiving team wins the rally, it receives a point which is recorded on the line of the next server's number and a square is drawn around it. Also draw a square around the same point on the team's running score. Draw a triangle around serve order position in which the Libero serves and around all points score by the Libero.

Date:	Location:		Start Time:	Finish Time:
Home Team:	Visitor Team:		Game No.:	Level:

Time-Outs		TEAM:				First Serve		Time-Outs		TEAM:	

| Serve Order | Player No. | Libero # : | | | | | | | | Running Score | | Serve Order | Player No. | Libero # : | | | | | | |

Running Score columns:
1 17 | 1 17
2 18 | 2 18
3 19 | 3 19
4 20 | 4 20
5 21 | 5 21
6 22 | 6 22
7 23 | 7 23
8 24 | 8 24
9 25 | 9 25
10 26 | 10 26
11 27 | 11 27
12 28 | 12 28
13 29 | 13 29
14 30 | 14 30
15 31 | 15 31
16 32 | 16 32

Serve Order rows: I, II, III, IV, V, VI (both teams)

Substitutions: 1 2 3 4 5 6 7 8 9 10 11 12 13 14 15 16 17 18   **Substitutions:** 1 2 3 4 5 6 7 8 9 10 11 12 13 14 15 16 17 18

Comments: Final Score   **Comments:**

REFEREE'S VERIFICATION		SCOREKEEPER	
FIRST REFEREE		WINNING TEAM	
SECOND REFEREE		LOSING TEAM	

KEYS:

C = Playing Captain
S = Substitution
Sx = Substitution Opponent

⊣ = Loss Of Rally
R = Replay
RS = Re-Serve

T = Time-Out
Tx = Time-Out Opponent
1,2,3..etc = General Point

P1, P2, P3 = Penalty Point
Px = Penalty Opponent
☐ = Point Scored Off Loss Of Rally
△ = Libero Point

If the receiving team wins the rally, it receives a point which is recorded on the line of the next server's number and a square is drawn around it. Also draw a square around the same point on the team's running score. Draw a triangle around serve order position in which the Libero serves and around all points score by the Libero.

Date:	Location:		Start Time:	Finish Time:
Home Team:	Visitor Team:		Game No.:	Level:

Time-Outs		TEAM:		First Serve		Time-Outs		TEAM:	
				Running Score					

Serve Order	Player No.	Libero # :			1	17	1	17	Serve Order	Player No.	Libero # :	
					2	18	2	18				
I					3	19	3	19	I			
					4	20	4	20				
II					5	21	5	21	II			
					6	22	6	22				
III					7	23	7	23	III			
					8	24	8	24				
IV					9	25	9	25	IV			
					10	26	10	26				
V					11	27	11	27	V			
					12	28	12	28				
VI					13	29	13	29	VI			
					14	30	14	30				
					15	31	15	31				

Substitutions: 1 2 3 4 5 6 7 8 9 10 11 12 13 14 15 16 17 18   16 | 32 | 16 | 32   Substitutions: 1 2 3 4 5 6 7 8 9 10 11 12 13 14 15 16 17 18

Comments: Final Score   Comments:

REFEREE'S VERIFICATION		SCOREKEEPER	
FIRST REFEREE		WINNING TEAM	
SECOND REFEREE		LOSING TEAM	

KEYS:

C = Playing Captain   ⊣ = Loss Of Rally   T = Time-Out   P1, P2, P3 = Penalty Point

S = Substitution   R = Replay   Tx = Time-Out Opponent   Px = Penalty Opponent

Sx = Substitution Opponent   RS = Re-Serve   1,2,3..etc = General Point   ☐ = Point Scored Off Loss Of Rally

△ = Libero Point

If the receiving team wins the rally, it receives a point which is recorded on the line of the next server's number and a square is drawn around it. Also draw a square around the same point on the team's running score. Draw a triangle around serve order position in which the Libero serves and around all points score by the Libero.

Date:		Location:						Start Time:		Finish Time:	
Home Team:			Visitor Team:					Game No.:		Level:	

Time-Outs		TEAM:					First Serve		Time-Outs		TEAM:	

Left side

Serve Order	Player No.	Libero # :					
I		--------					
II		--------					
III		--------					
IV		--------					
V		--------					
VI		--------					

Running Score (center)

1 17	1 17	Serve Order
2 18	2 18	I
3 19	3 19	
4 20	4 20	
5 21	5 21	II
6 22	6 22	
7 23	7 23	III
8 24	8 24	
9 25	9 25	IV
10 26	10 26	
11 27	11 27	V
12 28	12 28	
13 29	13 29	
14 30	14 30	VI
15 31	15 31	
16 32	16 32	

Right side

Player No.	Libero # :					

Substitutions: 1 2 3 4 5 6 7 8 9 10 11 12 13 14 15 16 17 18

Comments:

Substitutions: 1 2 3 4 5 6 7 8 9 10 11 12 13 14 15 16 17 18

Final Score

Comments:

REFEREE'S VERIFICATION		SCOREKEEPER	
FIRST REFEREE		WINNING TEAM	
SECOND REFEREE		LOSING TEAM	

KEYS:

C = Playing Captain

S = Substitution

Sx = Substitution Opponent

—| = Loss Of Rally

R = Replay

RS = Re-Serve

T = Time-Out

Tx = Time-Out Opponent

1,2,3..etc = General Point

P1, P2, P3 = Penalty Point

Px = Penalty Opponent

☐ = Point Scored Off Loss Of Rally

△ = Libero Point

If the receiving team wins the rally, it receives a point which is recorded on the line of the next server's number and a square is drawn around it. Also draw a square around the same point on the team's running score. Draw a triangle around serve order position in which the Libero serves and around all points score by the Libero.

Date:	Location:		Start Time:	Finish Time:

Home Team:	Visitor Team:	Game No.:	Level:

Time-Outs	TEAM:				First Serve		Time-Outs	TEAM:	
					Running Score				

Serve Order	Player No.	Libero # :				1 17	1 17	Serve Order	Player No.	Libero # :
						2 18	2 18			
I						3 19	3 19	I		
						4 20	4 20			
II						5 21	5 21	II		
						6 22	6 22			
III						7 23	7 23	III		
						8 24	8 24			
IV						9 25	9 25	IV		
						10 26	10 26			
V						11 27	11 27	V		
						12 28	12 28			
						13 29	13 29			
VI						14 30	14 30	VI		
						15 31	15 31			

Substitutions: 1 2 3 4 5 6 7 8 9 10 11 12 13 14 15 16 17 18 | 16 32 | 16 32 | Substitutions: 1 2 3 4 5 6 7 8 9 10 11 12 13 14 15 16 17 18

Comments:

Final Score | Comments:

REFEREE'S VERIFICATION		SCOREKEEPER	
FIRST REFEREE		WINNING TEAM	
SECOND REFEREE		LOSING TEAM	

KEYS:

C = Playing Captain   —| = Loss Of Rally   T = Time-Out   P1, P2, P3 = Penalty Point

S = Substitution   R = Replay   Tx = Time-Out Opponent   Px = Penalty Opponent

Sx = Substitution Opponent   RS = Re-Serve   1,2,3..etc = General Point   ☐ = Point Scored Off Loss Of Rally

△ = Libero Point

If the receiving team wins the rally, it receives a point which is recorded on the line of the next server's number and a square is drawn around it. Also draw a square around the same point on the team's running score. Draw a triangle around serve order position in which the Libero serves and around all points score by the Libero.

Date:		Location:				Start Time:		Finish Time:	
Home Team:			Visitor Team:			Game No.:		Level:	

Time-Outs		TEAM:		First Serve	Time-Outs		TEAM:	
				Running Score				

Serve Order	Player No.	Libero # :		1 : 17	1 : 17	Serve Order	Player No.	Libero # :
				2 : 18	2 : 18			
I				3 : 19	3 : 19	I		
				4 : 20	4 : 20			
II				5 : 21	5 : 21	II		
				6 : 22	6 : 22			
III				7 : 23	7 : 23	III		
				8 : 24	8 : 24			
IV				9 : 25	9 : 25	IV		
				10 : 26	10 : 26			
V				11 : 27	11 : 27	V		
				12 : 28	12 : 28			
				13 : 29	13 : 29			
VI				14 : 30	14 : 30	VI		
				15 : 31	15 : 31			

Substitutions: 1 2 3 4 5 6 7 8 9 10 11 12 13 14 15 16 17 18 | 16 : 32 | 16 : 32 | Substitutions: 1 2 3 4 5 6 7 8 9 10 11 12 13 14 15 16 17 18

Comments: | Final Score | Comments:

REFEREE'S VERIFICATION		SCOREKEEPER	
FIRST REFEREE		WINNING TEAM	
SECOND REFEREE		LOSING TEAM	

KEYS:

C = Playing Captain
S = Substitution
Sx = Substitution Opponent

—| = Loss Of Rally
R = Replay
RS = Re-Serve

T = Time-Out
Tx = Time-Out Opponent
1,2,3..etc = General Point

P1, P2, P3 = Penalty Point
Px = Penalty Opponent
☐ = Point Scored Off Loss Of Rally
△ = Libero Point

If the receiving team wins the rally, it receives a point which is recorded on the line of the next server's number and a square is drawn around it. Also draw a square around the same point on the team's running score. Draw a triangle around serve order position in which the Libero serves and around all points score by the Libero.

Date:		Location:				Start Time:		Finish Time:	
Home Team:			Visitor Team:			Game No.:		Level:	

Time-Outs		TEAM:											First Serve		Time-Outs		TEAM:											

Running Score

Serve Order	Player No.	Libero # :											Running Score		Serve Order	Player No.	Libero # :											

Running Score columns:
1 17 1 17
2 18 2 18
3 19 3 19
4 20 4 20
5 21 5 21
6 22 6 22
7 23 7 23
8 24 8 24
9 25 9 25
10 26 10 26
11 27 11 27
12 28 12 28
13 29 13 29
14 30 14 30
15 31 15 31
16 32 16 32

Serve Order rows: I, II, III, IV, V, VI (both sides)

Substitutions: 1 2 3 4 5 6 7 8 9 10 11 12 13 14 15 16 17 18 | 16 32 16 32 | Substitutions: 1 2 3 4 5 6 7 8 9 10 11 12 13 14 15 16 17 18

Comments: | Final Score | Comments:

REFEREE'S VERIFICATION		SCOREKEEPER	
FIRST REFEREE		WINNING TEAM	
SECOND REFEREE		LOSING TEAM	

KEYS:

C = Playing Captain   ⊣ = Loss Of Rally   T = Time-Out   P1, P2, P3 = Penalty Point

S = Substitution   R = Replay   Tx = Time-Out Opponent   Px = Penalty Opponent

Sx = Substitution Opponent   RS = Re-Serve   1,2,3..etc = General Point   ☐ = Point Scored Off Loss Of Rally

△ = Libero Point

If the receiving team wins the rally, it receives a point which is recorded on the line of the next server's number and a square is drawn around it. Also draw a square around the same point on the team's running score. Draw a triangle around serve order position in which the Libero serves and around all points score by the Libero.

| Date: | | Location: | | | Start Time: | | Finish Time: | |

| Home Team: | | Visitor Team: | | Game No.: | | Level: | |

<table>
<tr><td colspan="2">Time-Outs</td><td rowspan="2">TEAM:</td><td colspan="2">First Serve</td><td colspan="2">Time-Outs</td><td rowspan="2">TEAM:</td></tr>
<tr><td></td><td></td><td colspan="2">Running Score</td><td></td><td></td></tr>
<tr><td>Serve Order</td><td>Player No.</td><td>Libero # :</td><td>1 17 1 17
2 18 2 18</td><td>Serve Order</td><td>Player No.</td><td>Libero # :</td></tr>
</table>

Serve Order / Running Score columns:

1	17	1	17
2	18	2	18
3	19	3	19
4	20	4	20
5	21	5	21
6	22	6	22
7	23	7	23
8	24	8	24
9	25	9	25
10	26	10	26
11	27	11	27
12	28	12	28
13	29	13	29
14	30	14	30
15	31	15	31
16	32	16	32

Serve Order (left team): I, II, III, IV, V, VI
Serve Order (right team): I, II, III, IV, V, VI

Substitutions: 1 2 3 4 5 6 7 8 9 10 11 12 13 14 15 16 17 18

Final Score

Substitutions: 1 2 3 4 5 6 7 8 9 10 11 12 13 14 15 16 17 18

Comments:

Comments:

REFEREE'S VERIFICATION		SCOREKEEPER	
FIRST REFEREE		WINNING TEAM	
SECOND REFEREE		LOSING TEAM	

KEYS:

C = Playing Captain	—| = Loss Of Rally	T = Time-Out	P1, P2, P3 = Penalty Point	
S = Substitution	R = Replay	Tx = Time-Out Opponent	Px = Penalty Opponent	
Sx = Substitution Opponent	RS = Re-Serve	1,2,3..etc = General Point	☐ = Point Scored Off Loss Of Rally	
			△ = Libero Point	

If the receiving team wins the rally, it receives a point which is recorded on the line of the next server's number and a square is drawn around it. Also draw a square around the same point on the team's running score. Draw a triangle around serve order position in which the Libero serves and around all points score by the Libero.

Date:	Location:		Start Time:	Finish Time:
Home Team:	Visitor Team:		Game No.:	Level:

Time-Outs		TEAM:						First Serve		Time-Outs		TEAM:
								Running Score				

Serve Order	Player No.	Libero # :						1 17	1 17	Serve Order	Player No.	Libero # :
								2 18	2 18			
I								3 19	3 19	I		
								4 20	4 20			
II								5 21	5 21	II		
								6 22	6 22			
III								7 23	7 23	III		
								8 24	8 24			
IV								9 25	9 25	IV		
								10 26	10 26			
V								11 27	11 27	V		
								12 28	12 28			
								13 29	13 29			
VI								14 30	14 30	VI		
								15 31	15 31			

Substitutions: 1 2 3 4 5 6 7 8 9 10 11 12 13 14 15 16 17 18 | 16 32 | 16 32 | Substitutions: 1 2 3 4 5 6 7 8 9 10 11 12 13 14 15 16 17 18

Comments:	Final Score	Comments:

REFEREE'S VERIFICATION		SCOREKEEPER	
FIRST REFEREE		WINNING TEAM	
SECOND REFEREE		LOSING TEAM	

KEYS:

C = Playing Captain   ⊣ = Loss Of Rally   T = Time-Out   P1, P2, P3 = Penalty Point

S = Substitution   R = Replay   Tx = Time-Out Opponent   Px = Penalty Opponent

Sx = Substitution Opponent   RS = Re-Serve   1,2,3..etc = General Point   ☐ = Point Scored Off Loss Of Rally

△ = Libero Point

If the receiving team wins the rally, it receives a point which is recorded on the line of the next server's number and a square is drawn around it. Also draw a square around the same point on the team's running score. Draw a triangle around serve order position in which the Libero serves and around all points score by the Libero.

Date:	Location:		Start Time:	Finish Time:
Home Team:	Visitor Team:		Game No.:	Level:

Time-Outs		TEAM:		First Serve	Time-Outs		TEAM:	

Running Score

Serve Order	Player No.	Libero # :	1 17 1 17	Serve Order	Player No.	Libero # :
			2 18 2 18			
I			3 19 3 19	I		
			4 20 4 20			
II			5 21 5 21	II		
			6 22 6 22			
III			7 23 7 23	III		
			8 24 8 24			
IV			9 25 9 25	IV		
			10 26 10 26			
V			11 27 11 27	V		
			12 28 12 28			
VI			13 29 13 29	VI		
			14 30 14 30			
			15 31 15 31			

Substitutions: 1 2 3 4 5 6 7 8 9 10 11 12 13 14 15 16 17 18 | 16 32 16 32 | Substitutions: 1 2 3 4 5 6 7 8 9 10 11 12 13 14 15 16 17 18

Comments: | Final Score | Comments:

REFEREE'S VERIFICATION		SCOREKEEPER	
FIRST REFEREE		WINNING TEAM	
SECOND REFEREE		LOSING TEAM	

KEYS:

C = Playing Captain —| = Loss Of Rally T = Time-Out P1, P2, P3 = Penalty Point
S = Substitution R = Replay Tx = Time-Out Opponent Px = Penalty Opponent
Sx = Substitution Opponent RS = Re-Serve 1,2,3..etc = General Point □ = Point Scored Off Loss Of Rally
△ = Libero Point

If the receiving team wins the rally, it receives a point which is recorded on the line of the next server's number and a square is drawn around it. Also draw a square around the same point on the team's running score. Draw a triangle around serve order position in which the Libero serves and around all points score by the Libero.

Date:	Location:		Start Time:	Finish Time:

Home Team:	Visitor Team:	Game No.:	Level:

Time-Outs		TEAM:						First Serve		Time-Outs		TEAM:						
								Running Score										
Serve Order	Player No.	Libero # :						1 ¦ 17 1 ¦17		Serve Order	Player No.	Libero # :						
								2 ¦ 18 2 ¦18										
I								3 ¦ 19 3 ¦19		I								
								4 ¦ 20 4 ¦20										
II								5 ¦ 21 5 ¦21		II								
								6 ¦ 22 6 ¦22										
III								7 ¦ 23 7 ¦23		III								
								8 ¦ 24 8 ¦24										
IV								9 ¦ 25 9 ¦25		IV								
								10 ¦26 10 ¦26										
V								11 ¦27 11 ¦27		V								
								12 ¦28 12 ¦28										
								13 ¦29 13 ¦29										
VI								14 ¦30 14 ¦30		VI								
								15 ¦31 15 ¦31										

Substitutions:1 2 3 4 5 6 7 8 9 10 11 12 13 14 15 16 17 18	16 ¦32 16 ¦32	Substitutions:1 2 3 4 5 6 7 8 9 10 11 12 13 14 15 16 17 18
Comments:	Final Score	Comments:

REFEREE'S VERIFICATION		SCOREKEEPER	
FIRST REFEREE		WINNING TEAM	
SECOND REFEREE		LOSING TEAM	

KEYS:

C = Playing Captain   —| = Loss Of Rally   T = Time-Out   P1, P2, P3 = Penalty Point
S = Substitution   R = Replay   Tx = Time-Out Opponent   Px = Penalty Opponent
Sx = Substitution Opponent   RS = Re-Serve   1,2,3..etc = General Point   ☐ = Point Scored Off Loss Of Rally
△ = Libero Point

If the receiving team wins the rally, it receives a point which is recorded on the line of the next server's number and a square is drawn around it. Also draw a square around the same point on the team's running score. Draw a triangle around serve order position in which the Libero serves and around all points score by the Libero.

Date:	Location:		Start Time:	Finish Time:
Home Team:		Visitor Team:	Game No.:	Level:

Time-Outs	TEAM:		First Serve	Time-Outs	TEAM:

Running Score

Serve Order	Player No.	Libero # :										1 17 1 17	Serve Order	Player No.	Libero # :
												2 18 2 18			
I												3 19 3 19	I		
												4 20 4 20			
II												5 21 5 21	II		
												6 22 6 22			
III												7 23 7 23	III		
												8 24 8 24			
IV												9 25 9 25	IV		
												10 26 10 26			
V												11 27 11 27	V		
												12 28 12 28			
												13 29 13 29			
VI												14 30 14 30	VI		
												15 31 15 31			

Substitutions: 1 2 3 4 5 6 7 8 9 10 11 12 13 14 15 16 17 18 | **16 32 16 32** | Substitutions: 1 2 3 4 5 6 7 8 9 10 11 12 13 14 15 16 17 18

Comments: | **Final Score** | Comments:

REFEREE'S VERIFICATION		SCOREKEEPER	
FIRST REFEREE		WINNING TEAM	
SECOND REFEREE		LOSING TEAM	

KEYS:

C = Playing Captain
S = Substitution
Sx = Substitution Opponent

▬| = Loss Of Rally
R = Replay
RS = Re-Serve

T = Time-Out
Tx = Time-Out Opponent
1,2,3..etc = General Point

P1, P2, P3 = Penalty Point
Px = Penalty Opponent
▢ = Point Scored Off Loss Of Rally
△ = Libero Point

If the receiving team wins the rally, it receives a point which is recorded on the line of the next server's number and a square is drawn around it. Also draw a square around the same point on the team's running score. Draw a triangle around serve order position in which the Libero serves and around all points score by the Libero.

Date:	Location:		Start Time:	Finish Time:

Home Team:	Visitor Team:	Game No.:	Level:

Time-Outs		TEAM:		First Serve			Time-Outs		TEAM:	

Running Score

Serve Order	Player No.	Libero # :		1	17	1	17	Serve Order	Player No.	Libero # :
				2	18	2	18			
I				3	19	3	19	I		
				4	20	4	20			
II				5	21	5	21	II		
				6	22	6	22			
III				7	23	7	23	III		
				8	24	8	24			
IV				9	25	9	25	IV		
				10	26	10	26			
V				11	27	11	27	V		
				12	28	12	28			
				13	29	13	29			
VI				14	30	14	30	VI		
				15	31	15	31			

Substitutions: 1 2 3 4 5 6 7 8 9 10 11 12 13 14 15 16 17 18	16	32	16	32	Substitutions: 1 2 3 4 5 6 7 8 9 10 11 12 13 14 15 16 17 18

Comments:	Final Score	Comments:

REFEREE'S VERIFICATION		SCOREKEEPER	
FIRST REFEREE		WINNING TEAM	
SECOND REFEREE		LOSING TEAM	

KEYS:

C = Playing Captain

S = Substitution

Sx = Substitution Opponent

▬| = Loss Of Rally

R = Replay

RS = Re-Serve

T = Time-Out

Tx = Time-Out Opponent

1,2,3..etc = General Point

P1, P2, P3 = Penalty Point

Px = Penalty Opponent

☐ = Point Scored Off Loss Of Rally

△ = Libero Point

If the receiving team wins the rally, it receives a point which is recorded on the line of the next server's number and a square is drawn around it. Also draw a square around the same point on the team's running score. Draw a triangle around serve order position in which the Libero serves and around all points score by the Libero.

Date:		Location:						Start Time:		Finish Time:	

Home Team:		Visitor Team:				Game No.:		Level:	

Time-Outs | TEAM: | | First Serve | Time-Outs | TEAM:

Time-Outs		TEAM:				First Serve	Time-Outs		TEAM:	

Running Score

Serve Order	Player No.	Libero # :										1 17 1 17 2 18 2 18	Serve Order	Player No.	Libero # :									

| I | | -------- | | | | | | | | | | 3 19 3 19
4 20 4 20 | I | | -------- | | | | | | | | | |

| II | | -------- | | | | | | | | | | 5 21 5 21
6 22 6 22 | II | | -------- | | | | | | | | | |

| III | | -------- | | | | | | | | | | 7 23 7 23
8 24 8 24 | III | | -------- | | | | | | | | | |

| IV | | -------- | | | | | | | | | | 9 25 9 25
10 26 10 26 | IV | | -------- | | | | | | | | | |

| V | | -------- | | | | | | | | | | 11 27 11 27
12 28 12 28 | V | | -------- | | | | | | | | | |

| VI | | -------- | | | | | | | | | | 13 29 13 29
14 30 14 30
15 31 15 31 | VI | | -------- | | | | | | | | | |

Substitutions: 1 2 3 4 5 6 7 8 9 10 11 12 13 14 15 16 17 18 | 16 32 16 32 | Substitutions: 1 2 3 4 5 6 7 8 9 10 11 12 13 14 15 16 17 18

Comments: | Final Score | Comments:

REFEREE'S VERIFICATION		SCOREKEEPER	
FIRST REFEREE		WINNING TEAM	
SECOND REFEREE		LOSING TEAM	

KEYS:

C = Playing Captain   ⌐| = Loss Of Rally   T = Time-Out   P1, P2, P3 = Penalty Point

S = Substitution   R = Replay   Tx = Time-Out Opponent   Px = Penalty Opponent

Sx = Substitution Opponent   RS = Re-Serve   1,2,3..etc = General Point   ☐ = Point Scored Off Loss Of Rally

△ = Libero Point

If the receiving team wins the rally, it receives a point which is recorded on the line of the next server's number and a square is drawn around it. Also draw a square around the same point on the team's running score. Draw a triangle around serve order position in which the Libero serves and around all points score by the Libero.

Date:		Location:			Start Time:		Finish Time:	
Home Team:			Visitor Team:			Game No.:		Level:

Time-Outs		TEAM:		First Serve	Time-Outs		TEAM:	

Running Score

Serve Order	Player No.	Libero # :		1 | 17	1 | 17	Serve Order	Player No.	Libero # :
I				2 | 18 / 3 | 19 / 4 | 20	2 | 18 / 3 | 19 / 4 | 20	I		
II				5 | 21 / 6 | 22	5 | 21 / 6 | 22	II		
III				7 | 23 / 8 | 24	7 | 23 / 8 | 24	III		
IV				9 | 25 / 10 | 26	9 | 25 / 10 | 26	IV		
V				11 | 27 / 12 | 28 / 13 | 29	11 | 27 / 12 | 28 / 13 | 29	V		
VI				14 | 30 / 15 | 31	14 | 30 / 15 | 31	VI		

Substitutions: 1 2 3 4 5 6 7 8 9 10 11 12 13 14 15 16 17 18 | 16 \| 32 | 16 \| 32 | Substitutions: 1 2 3 4 5 6 7 8 9 10 11 12 13 14 15 16 17 18

Comments: | Final Score | Comments:

REFEREE'S VERIFICATION		SCOREKEEPER	
FIRST REFEREE		WINNING TEAM	
SECOND REFEREE		LOSING TEAM	

KEYS:

C = Playing Captain
S = Substitution
Sx = Substitution Opponent

—| = Loss Of Rally
R = Replay
RS = Re-Serve

T = Time-Out
Tx = Time-Out Opponent
1,2,3..etc = General Point

P1, P2, P3 = Penalty Point
Px = Penalty Opponent
☐ = Point Scored Off Loss Of Rally
△ = Libero Point

If the receiving team wins the rally, it receives a point which is recorded on the line of the next server's number and a square is drawn around it. Also draw a square around the same point on the team's running score. Draw a triangle around serve order position in which the Libero serves and around all points score by the Libero.

Date:	Location:		Start Time:	Finish Time:
Home Team:	Visitor Team:		Game No.:	Level:

Time-Outs		TEAM:		First Serve		Time-Outs		TEAM:
				Running Score				

Serve Order	Player No.	Libero # :	First Serve	Serve Order	Player No.	Libero # :
I			1 17 | 1 17 2 18 | 2 18	I		
II			3 19 | 3 19 4 20 | 4 20 5 21 | 5 21 6 22 | 6 22	II		
III			7 23 | 7 23 8 24 | 8 24	III		
IV			9 25 | 9 25 10 26 | 10 26	IV		
V			11 27 | 11 27 12 28 | 12 28 13 29 | 13 29	V		
VI			14 30 | 14 30 15 31 | 15 31 16 32 | 16 32	VI		

Substitutions: 1 2 3 4 5 6 7 8 9 10 11 12 13 14 15 16 17 18 | **Substitutions:** 1 2 3 4 5 6 7 8 9 10 11 12 13 14 15 16 17 18

Comments: | Final Score | **Comments:**

REFEREE'S VERIFICATION		SCOREKEEPER	
FIRST REFEREE		WINNING TEAM	
SECOND REFEREE		LOSING TEAM	

KEYS:

C = Playing Captain
S = Substitution
Sx = Substitution Opponent

▬| = Loss Of Rally
R = Replay
RS = Re-Serve

T = Time-Out
Tx = Time-Out Opponent
1,2,3..etc = General Point

P1, P2, P3 = Penalty Point
Px = Penalty Opponent
☐ = Point Scored Off Loss Of Rally
△ = Libero Point

If the receiving team wins the rally, it receives a point which is recorded on the line of the next server's number and a square is drawn around it. Also draw a square around the same point on the team's running score. Draw a triangle around serve order position in which the Libero serves and around all points score by the Libero.

Date:	Location:		Start Time:	Finish Time:

Home Team:	Visitor Team:	Game No.:	Level:

Time-Outs | **TEAM:** | **First Serve** | **Time-Outs** | **TEAM:**

Serve Order	Player No.	Libero # :											Running Score	Serve Order	Player No.	Libero # :											
													1 17 1 17														
													2 18 2 18														
I													3 19 3 19	I													
													4 20 4 20														
II													5 21 5 21	II													
													6 22 6 22														
III													7 23 7 23	III													
													8 24 8 24														
IV													9 25 9 25	IV													
													10 26 10 26														
V													11 27 11 27	V													
													12 28 12 28														
													13 29 13 29														
VI													14 30 14 30	VI													
													15 31 15 31														

Substitutions: 1 2 3 4 5 6 7 8 9 10 11 12 13 14 15 16 17 18 | 16 32 16 32 | Substitutions: 1 2 3 4 5 6 7 8 9 10 11 12 13 14 15 16 17 18

Comments: | **Final Score** | Comments:

REFEREE'S VERIFICATION		SCOREKEEPER	
FIRST REFEREE		WINNING TEAM	
SECOND REFEREE		LOSING TEAM	

KEYS:

C = Playing Captain   ⊣ = Loss Of Rally   T = Time-Out   P1, P2, P3 = Penalty Point

S = Substitution   R = Replay   Tx = Time-Out Opponent   Px = Penalty Opponent

Sx = Substitution Opponent   RS = Re-Serve   1,2,3..etc = General Point   ☐ = Point Scored Off Loss Of Rally

△ = Libero Point

If the receiving team wins the rally, it receives a point which is recorded on the line of the next server's number and a square is drawn around it. Also draw a square around the same point on the team's running score. Draw a triangle around serve order position in which the Libero serves and around all points score by the Libero.

Date:		Location:							Start Time:		Finish Time:	
Home Team:			Visitor Team:						Game No.:		Level:	

Time-Outs		TEAM:				First Serve				Time-Outs		TEAM:	
						Running Score							

TEAM (Home) — Serve Order / Player No. / Libero # :

First Serve — Running Score

1 ¦ 17	1 ¦ 17	
2 ¦ 18	2 ¦ 18	
3 ¦ 19	3 ¦ 19	
4 ¦ 20	4 ¦ 20	
5 ¦ 21	5 ¦ 21	
6 ¦ 22	6 ¦ 22	
7 ¦ 23	7 ¦ 23	
8 ¦ 24	8 ¦ 24	
9 ¦ 25	9 ¦ 25	
10 ¦ 26	10 ¦ 26	
11 ¦ 27	11 ¦ 27	
12 ¦ 28	12 ¦ 28	
13 ¦ 29	13 ¦ 29	
14 ¦ 30	14 ¦ 30	
15 ¦ 31	15 ¦ 31	
16 ¦ 32	16 ¦ 32	

Serve Order (Home): I, II, III, IV, V, VI

Serve Order (Visitor): I, II, III, IV, V, VI — Player No. / Libero # :

Substitutions: 1 2 3 4 5 6 7 8 9 10 11 12 13 14 15 16 17 18

Comments:

Substitutions: 1 2 3 4 5 6 7 8 9 10 11 12 13 14 15 16 17 18

Comments:

Final Score

REFEREE'S VERIFICATION		SCOREKEEPER	
FIRST REFEREE		WINNING TEAM	
SECOND REFEREE		LOSING TEAM	

KEYS:

C = Playing Captain
S = Substitution
Sx = Substitution Opponent

—| = Loss Of Rally
R = Replay
RS = Re-Serve

T = Time-Out
Tx = Time-Out Opponent
1,2,3..etc = General Point

P1, P2, P3 = Penalty Point
Px = Penalty Opponent
☐ = Point Scored Off Loss Of Rally
△ = Libero Point

If the receiving team wins the rally, it receives a point which is recorded on the line of the next server's number and a square is drawn around it. Also draw a square around the same point on the team's running score. Draw a triangle around serve order position in which the Libero serves and around all points score by the Libero.

Date:	Location:		Start Time:	Finish Time:

Home Team:	Visitor Team:	Game No.:	Level:

Time-Outs	TEAM:		First Serve	Time-Outs	TEAM:

Running Score

Serve Order	Player No.	Libero # :							1 ¦ 17	1 ¦ 17	Serve Order	Player No.	Libero # :									
									2 ¦ 18	2 ¦ 18												
I									3 ¦ 19	3 ¦ 19	I											
									4 ¦ 20	4 ¦ 20												
II									5 ¦ 21	5 ¦ 21	II											
									6 ¦ 22	6 ¦ 22												
III									7 ¦ 23	7 ¦ 23	III											
									8 ¦ 24	8 ¦ 24												
IV									9 ¦ 25	9 ¦ 25	IV											
									10 ¦ 26	10 ¦ 26												
V									11 ¦ 27	11 ¦ 27	V											
									12 ¦ 28	12 ¦ 28												
									13 ¦ 29	13 ¦ 29												
VI									14 ¦ 30	14 ¦ 30	VI											
									15 ¦ 31	15 ¦ 31												

Substitutions:1 2 3 4 5 6 7 8 9 10 11 12 13 14 15 16 17 18	16 ¦ 32	16 ¦ 32	Substitutions:1 2 3 4 5 6 7 8 9 10 11 12 13 14 15 16 17 18

Comments:	Final Score	Comments:

REFEREE'S VERIFICATION		SCOREKEEPER	
FIRST REFEREE		WINNING TEAM	
SECOND REFEREE		LOSING TEAM	

KEYS:

C = Playing Captain   ▬| = Loss Of Rally   T = Time-Out   P1, P2, P3 = Penalty Point

S = Substitution   R = Replay   Tx = Time-Out Opponent   Px = Penalty Opponent

Sx = Substitution Opponent   RS = Re-Serve   1,2,3..etc = General Point   □ = Point Scored Off Loss Of Rally

△ = Libero Point

If the receiving team wins the rally, it receives a point which is recorded on the line of the next server's number and a square is drawn around it. Also draw a square around the same point on the team's running score. Draw a triangle around serve order position in which the Libero serves and around all points score by the Libero.

Date:		Location:					Start Time:		Finish Time:	

Home Team:		Visitor Team:			Game No.:		Level:	

Time-Outs		TEAM:			First Serve		Time-Outs		TEAM:	

					Running Score					
Serve Order	Player No.	Libero # :			1 17 1 17		Serve Order	Player No.	Libero # :	
I					2 18 2 18		I			
					3 19 3 19					
					4 20 4 20					
II					5 21 5 21		II			
					6 22 6 22					
III					7 23 7 23		III			
					8 24 8 24					
IV					9 25 9 25		IV			
					10 26 10 26					
V					11 27 11 27		V			
					12 28 12 28					
					13 29 13 29					
VI					14 30 14 30		VI			
					15 31 15 31					

Substitutions: 1 2 3 4 5 6 7 8 9 10 11 12 13 14 15 16 17 18 | 16 32 16 32 | Substitutions: 1 2 3 4 5 6 7 8 9 10 11 12 13 14 15 16 17 18

Comments: | Final Score | Comments:

REFEREE'S VERIFICATION		SCOREKEEPER	
FIRST REFEREE		WINNING TEAM	
SECOND REFEREE		LOSING TEAM	

KEYS:

C = Playing Captain

S = Substitution

Sx = Substitution Opponent

⊣ = Loss Of Rally

R = Replay

RS = Re-Serve

T = Time-Out

Tx = Time-Out Opponent

1,2,3..etc = General Point

P1, P2, P3 = Penalty Point

Px = Penalty Opponent

☐ = Point Scored Off Loss Of Rally

△ = Libero Point

If the receiving team wins the rally, it receives a point which is recorded on the line of the next server's number and a square is drawn around it. Also draw a square around the same point on the team's running score. Draw a triangle around serve order position in which the Libero serves and around all points score by the Libero.

Date:	Location:		Start Time:	Finish Time:
Home Team:	Visitor Team:		Game No.:	Level:

Time-Outs		TEAM:		First Serve	Time-Outs		TEAM:

| | | | | Running Score | | | |

TEAM: Libero # :

| Serve Order | Player No. | Libero # : | | | | | | | | | | | | | Running Score | Serve Order | Player No. | Libero # : |

Serve Order													
I													
II													
III													
IV													
V													
VI													

Running Score column:
1 17 1 17
2 18 2 18
3 19 3 19
4 20 4 20
5 21 5 21
6 22 6 22
7 23 7 23
8 24 8 24
9 25 9 25
10 26 10 26
11 27 11 27
12 28 12 28
13 29 13 29
14 30 14 30
15 31 15 31
16 32 16 32

Right team serve order: I, II, III, IV, V, VI

Substitutions: 1 2 3 4 5 6 7 8 9 10 11 12 13 14 15 16 17 18

Final Score

Substitutions: 1 2 3 4 5 6 7 8 9 10 11 12 13 14 15 16 17 18

Comments:

Comments:

REFEREE'S VERIFICATION		SCOREKEEPER	
FIRST REFEREE		WINNING TEAM	
SECOND REFEREE		LOSING TEAM	

KEYS:

C = Playing Captain
S = Substitution
Sx = Substitution Opponent

—| = Loss Of Rally
R = Replay
RS = Re-Serve

T = Time-Out
Tx = Time-Out Opponent
1,2,3..etc = General Point

P1, P2, P3 = Penalty Point
Px = Penalty Opponent
□ = Point Scored Off Loss Of Rally
△ = Libero Point

If the receiving team wins the rally, it receives a point which is recorded on the line of the next server's number and a square is drawn around it. Also draw a square around the same point on the team's running score. Draw a triangle around serve order position in which the Libero serves and around all points score by the Libero.

Date:		Location:						Start Time:		Finish Time:	
Home Team:			Visitor Team:					Game No.:		Level:	

Time-Outs		TEAM:							First Serve			Time-Outs		TEAM:							

First Serve / Running Score

Serve Order	Player No.	Libero # :								Running Score		Serve Order	Player No.	Libero # :								

Running Score columns:
1	17	1	17
2	18	2	18
3	19	3	19
4	20	4	20
5	21	5	21
6	22	6	22
7	23	7	23
8	24	8	24
9	25	9	25
10	26	10	26
11	27	11	27
12	28	12	28
13	29	13	29
14	30	14	30
15	31	15	31
16	32	16	32

Serve order positions (left and right): I, II, III, IV, V, VI

Substitutions: 1 2 3 4 5 6 7 8 9 10 11 12 13 14 15 16 17 18

Comments:

Final Score

Substitutions: 1 2 3 4 5 6 7 8 9 10 11 12 13 14 15 16 17 18

Comments:

REFEREE'S VERIFICATION		SCOREKEEPER	
FIRST REFEREE		WINNING TEAM	
SECOND REFEREE		LOSING TEAM	

KEYS:

C = Playing Captain
S = Substitution
Sx = Substitution Opponent

—| = Loss Of Rally
R = Replay
RS = Re-Serve

T = Time-Out
Tx = Time-Out Opponent
1,2,3..etc = General Point

P1, P2, P3 = Penalty Point
Px = Penalty Opponent
☐ = Point Scored Off Loss Of Rally
△ = Libero Point

If the receiving team wins the rally, it receives a point which is recorded on the line of the next server's number and a square is drawn around it. Also draw a square around the same point on the team's running score. Draw a triangle around serve order position in which the Libero serves and around all points score by the Libero.

Date:	Location:		Start Time:	Finish Time:
Home Team:	Visitor Team:		Game No.:	Level:

Time-Outs		TEAM:		First Serve		Time-Outs		TEAM:	
				Running Score					

Serve Order	Player No.	Libero # :	1	17	1	17	Serve Order	Player No.	Libero # :
			2	18	2	18			
I			3	19	3	19	I		
			4	20	4	20			
II			5	21	5	21	II		
			6	22	6	22			
III			7	23	7	23	III		
			8	24	8	24			
IV			9	25	9	25	IV		
			10	26	10	26			
V			11	27	11	27	V		
			12	28	12	28			
VI			13	29	13	29	VI		
			14	30	14	30			
			15	31	15	31			

Substitutions: 1 2 3 4 5 6 7 8 9 10 11 12 13 14 15 16 17 18 | 16 | 32 | 16 | 32 | Substitutions: 1 2 3 4 5 6 7 8 9 10 11 12 13 14 15 16 17 18

Comments: | Final Score | Comments:

REFEREE'S VERIFICATION		SCOREKEEPER	
FIRST REFEREE		WINNING TEAM	
SECOND REFEREE		LOSING TEAM	

KEYS:

C = Playing Captain
S = Substitution
Sx = Substitution Opponent

—| = Loss Of Rally
R = Replay
RS = Re-Serve

T = Time-Out
Tx = Time-Out Opponent
1,2,3..etc = General Point

P1, P2, P3 = Penalty Point
Px = Penalty Opponent
□ = Point Scored Off Loss Of Rally
△ = Libero Point

If the receiving team wins the rally, it receives a point which is recorded on the line of the next server's number and a square is drawn around it. Also draw a square around the same point on the team's running score. Draw a triangle around serve order position in which the Libero serves and around all points score by the Libero.

Date:	Location:		Start Time:	Finish Time:
Home Team:		Visitor Team:	Game No.:	Level:

Time-Outs		TEAM:		First Serve		Time-Outs		TEAM:

Running Score

Serve Order	Player No.	Libero # :		1 17 1 17	Serve Order	Player No.	Libero # :
I			2 18 2 18	I		
			3 19 3 19			
			4 20 4 20			
II			5 21 5 21	II		
			6 22 6 22			
III			7 23 7 23	III		
			8 24 8 24			
IV			9 25 9 25	IV		
			10 26 10 26			
V			11 27 11 27	V		
			12 28 12 28			
VI			13 29 13 29	VI		
			14 30 14 30			
			15 31 15 31			

Substitutions: 1 2 3 4 5 6 7 8 9 10 11 12 13 14 15 16 17 18 | 16 32 16 32 | Substitutions: 1 2 3 4 5 6 7 8 9 10 11 12 13 14 15 16 17 18

Comments: | Final Score | Comments:

REFEREE'S VERIFICATION		SCOREKEEPER	
FIRST REFEREE		WINNING TEAM	
SECOND REFEREE		LOSING TEAM	

KEYS:

C = Playing Captain   —| = Loss Of Rally   T = Time-Out   P1, P2, P3 = Penalty Point

S = Substitution   R = Replay   Tx = Time-Out Opponent   Px = Penalty Opponent

Sx = Substitution Opponent   RS = Re-Serve   1,2,3..etc = General Point   ☐ = Point Scored Off Loss Of Rally

△ = Libero Point

If the receiving team wins the rally, it receives a point which is recorded on the line of the next server's number and a square is drawn around it. Also draw a square around the same point on the team's running score. Draw a triangle around serve order position in which the Libero serves and around all points score by the Libero.

Date:	Location:		Start Time:	Finish Time:
Home Team:	Visitor Team:		Game No.:	Level:

Time-Outs	TEAM:	First Serve	Time-Outs	TEAM:

Running Score

Serve Order	Player No.	Libero # :											1 : 17	1 : 17	Serve Order	Player No.	Libero # :
													2 : 18	2 : 18			
I													3 : 19	3 : 19	I		
													4 : 20	4 : 20			
II													5 : 21	5 : 21	II		
													6 : 22	6 : 22			
III													7 : 23	7 : 23	III		
													8 : 24	8 : 24			
IV													9 : 25	9 : 25	IV		
													10 : 26	10 : 26			
V													11 : 27	11 : 27	V		
													12 : 28	12 : 28			
													13 : 29	13 : 29			
VI													14 : 30	14 : 30	VI		
													15 : 31	15 : 31			

Substitutions: 1 2 3 4 5 6 7 8 9 10 11 12 13 14 15 16 17 18 | 16 : 32 | 16 : 32 | Substitutions: 1 2 3 4 5 6 7 8 9 10 11 12 13 14 15 16 17 18

Comments: | Final Score | Comments:

REFEREE'S VERIFICATION		SCOREKEEPER	
FIRST REFEREE		WINNING TEAM	
SECOND REFEREE		LOSING TEAM	

KEYS:

C = Playing Captain
S = Substitution
Sx = Substitution Opponent

⊣ = Loss Of Rally
R = Replay
RS = Re-Serve

T = Time-Out
Tx = Time-Out Opponent
1,2,3..etc = General Point

P1, P2, P3 = Penalty Point
Px = Penalty Opponent
□ = Point Scored Off Loss Of Rally
△ = Libero Point

If the receiving team wins the rally, it receives a point which is recorded on the line of the next server's number and a square is drawn around it. Also draw a square around the same point on the team's running score. Draw a triangle around serve order position in which the Libero serves and around all points score by the Libero.

Date:		Location:					Start Time:		Finish Time:	
Home Team:			Visitor Team:				Game No.:		Level:	

Time-Outs		TEAM:							First Serve		Time-Outs		TEAM:				

Running Score

Serve Order	Player No.	Libero # :												1	17	1	17	Serve Order	Player No.	Libero # :

I — 2|18 2|18

II — 3|19 3|19 4|20 4|20

III — 5|21 5|21 6|22 6|22

IV — 7|23 7|23 8|24 8|24

V — 9|25 9|25 10|26 10|26

VI — 11|27 11|27 12|28 12|28

13|29 13|29
14|30 14|30
15|31 15|31

Substitutions: 1 2 3 4 5 6 7 8 9 10 11 12 13 14 15 16 17 18   16|32 16|32   **Substitutions:** 1 2 3 4 5 6 7 8 9 10 11 12 13 14 15 16 17 18

Comments: Final Score   **Comments:**

REFEREE'S VERIFICATION		SCOREKEEPER	
FIRST REFEREE		WINNING TEAM	
SECOND REFEREE		LOSING TEAM	

KEYS:

C = Playing Captain   ⊣ = Loss Of Rally   T = Time-Out   P1, P2, P3 = Penalty Point

S = Substitution   R = Replay   Tx = Time-Out Opponent   Px = Penalty Opponent

Sx = Substitution Opponent   RS = Re-Serve   1,2,3..etc = General Point   ☐ = Point Scored Off Loss Of Rally

△ = Libero Point

If the receiving team wins the rally, it receives a point which is recorded on the line of the next server's number and a square is drawn around it. Also draw a square around the same point on the team's running score. Draw a triangle around serve order position in which the Libero serves and around all points score by the Libero.

Date:	Location:		Start Time:	Finish Time:

Home Team:	Visitor Team:	Game No.:	Level:

Time-Outs		TEAM:		First Serve		Time-Outs		TEAM:

Running Score

Serve Order	Player No.	Libero # :	First Serve	Serve Order	Player No.	Libero # :

Running Score columns:
1	17	1	17
2	18	2	18
3	19	3	19
4	20	4	20
5	21	5	21
6	22	6	22
7	23	7	23
8	24	8	24
9	25	9	25
10	26	10	26
11	27	11	27
12	28	12	28
13	29	13	29
14	30	14	30
15	31	15	31
16	32	16	32

Serve order positions: I, II, III, IV, V, VI (both teams)

Substitutions: 1 2 3 4 5 6 7 8 9 10 11 12 13 14 15 16 17 18

Substitutions: 1 2 3 4 5 6 7 8 9 10 11 12 13 14 15 16 17 18

Comments:

Final Score

Comments:

REFEREE'S VERIFICATION		SCOREKEEPER	
FIRST REFEREE		WINNING TEAM	
SECOND REFEREE		LOSING TEAM	

KEYS:

C = Playing Captain
S = Substitution
Sx = Substitution Opponent

—| = Loss Of Rally
R = Replay
RS = Re-Serve

T = Time-Out
Tx = Time-Out Opponent
1,2,3..etc = General Point

P1, P2, P3 = Penalty Point
Px = Penalty Opponent
☐ = Point Scored Off Loss Of Rally
△ = Libero Point

If the receiving team wins the rally, it receives a point which is recorded on the line of the next server's number and a square is drawn around it. Also draw a square around the same point on the team's running score. Draw a triangle around serve order position in which the Libero serves and around all points score by the Libero.

Date:		Location:						Start Time:		Finish Time:	
Home Team:			Visitor Team:				Game No.:		Level:		

Time-Outs		TEAM:								First Serve		Time-Outs		TEAM:			
										Running Score							

Left Team

Serve Order	Player No.	Libero # :										
I												
II												
III												
IV												
V												
VI												

Running Score (center)

1	17	1	17
2	18	2	18
3	19	3	19
4	20	4	20
5	21	5	21
6	22	6	22
7	23	7	23
8	24	8	24
9	25	9	25
10	26	10	26
11	27	11	27
12	28	12	28
13	29	13	29
14	30	14	30
15	31	15	31
16	32	16	32

Right Team

Serve Order	Player No.	Libero # :										
I												
II												
III												
IV												
V												
VI												

Substitutions: 1 2 3 4 5 6 7 8 9 10 11 12 13 14 15 16 17 18

Substitutions: 1 2 3 4 5 6 7 8 9 10 11 12 13 14 15 16 17 18

Comments:

Final Score

Comments:

REFEREE'S VERIFICATION		SCOREKEEPER	
FIRST REFEREE		WINNING TEAM	
SECOND REFEREE		LOSING TEAM	

KEYS:

C = Playing Captain
S = Substitution
Sx = Substitution Opponent

━| = Loss Of Rally
R = Replay
RS = Re-Serve

T = Time-Out
Tx = Time-Out Opponent
1,2,3..etc = General Point

P1, P2, P3 = Penalty Point
Px = Penalty Opponent
☐ = Point Scored Off Loss Of Rally
△ = Libero Point

If the receiving team wins the rally, it receives a point which is recorded on the line of the next server's number and a square is drawn around it. Also draw a square around the same point on the team's running score. Draw a triangle around serve order position in which the Libero serves and around all points score by the Libero.

| Date: | | Location: | | | Start Time: | | Finish Time: | |

| Home Team: | | Visitor Team: | | Game No.: | | Level: | |

| Time-Outs | | TEAM: | | First Serve | | Time-Outs | | TEAM: |
| Running Score |

<table>
<tr><td colspan="2">Time-Outs</td><td rowspan="2">TEAM:</td><td colspan="2">First Serve</td><td colspan="2">Time-Outs</td><td>TEAM:</td></tr>
<tr><td colspan="2">Running Score</td></tr>
<tr><td>Serve Order</td><td>Player No.</td><td>Libero # :</td><td>1 | 17</td><td>1 | 17</td><td>Serve Order</td><td>Player No.</td><td>Libero # :</td></tr>
<tr><td rowspan="2">I</td><td></td><td></td><td>2 | 18</td><td>2 | 18</td><td rowspan="2">I</td><td></td><td></td></tr>
<tr><td></td><td></td><td>3 | 19</td><td>3 | 19</td><td></td><td></td></tr>
<tr><td rowspan="2">II</td><td></td><td></td><td>4 | 20</td><td>4 | 20</td><td rowspan="2">II</td><td></td><td></td></tr>
<tr><td></td><td></td><td>5 | 21</td><td>5 | 21</td><td></td><td></td></tr>
<tr><td rowspan="2">III</td><td></td><td></td><td>6 | 22</td><td>6 | 22</td><td rowspan="2">III</td><td></td><td></td></tr>
<tr><td></td><td></td><td>7 | 23</td><td>7 | 23</td><td></td><td></td></tr>
</table>

Serve Order / Player No. / Libero # :

I

II

III

IV

V

VI

First Serve — Running Score:
1 | 17   1 | 17
2 | 18   2 | 18
3 | 19   3 | 19
4 | 20   4 | 20
5 | 21   5 | 21
6 | 22   6 | 22
7 | 23   7 | 23
8 | 24   8 | 24
9 | 25   9 | 25
10 | 26   10 | 26
11 | 27   11 | 27
12 | 28   12 | 28
13 | 29   13 | 29
14 | 30   14 | 30
15 | 31   15 | 31
16 | 32   16 | 32

Substitutions: 1 2 3 4 5 6 7 8 9 10 11 12 13 14 15 16 17 18

Substitutions: 1 2 3 4 5 6 7 8 9 10 11 12 13 14 15 16 17 18

Comments:

Final Score

Comments:

REFEREE'S VERIFICATION		SCOREKEEPER	
FIRST REFEREE		WINNING TEAM	
SECOND REFEREE		LOSING TEAM	

KEYS:

C = Playing Captain
S = Substitution
Sx = Substitution Opponent

—| = Loss Of Rally
R = Replay
RS = Re-Serve

T = Time-Out
Tx = Time-Out Opponent
1,2,3..etc = General Point

P1, P2, P3 = Penalty Point
Px = Penalty Opponent
▢ = Point Scored Off Loss Of Rally
△ = Libero Point

If the receiving team wins the rally, it receives a point which is recorded on the line of the next server's number and a square is drawn around it. Also draw a square around the same point on the team's running score. Draw a triangle around serve order position in which the Libero serves and around all points score by the Libero.

Date:		Location:						Start Time:		Finish Time:	
Home Team:			Visitor Team:					Game No.:		Level:	

Time-Outs		TEAM:		First Serve		Time-Outs		TEAM:	

Running Score

Serve Order	Player No.	Libero # :		1 17 1 17	Serve Order	Player No.	Libero # :
				2 18 2 18			

I			3 19 3 19	I		
			4 20 4 20			
II			5 21 5 21	II		
			6 22 6 22			
III			7 23 7 23	III		
			8 24 8 24			
IV			9 25 9 25	IV		
			10 26 10 26			
V			11 27 11 27	V		
			12 28 12 28			
			13 29 13 29			
VI			14 30 14 30	VI		
			15 31 15 31			

Substitutions: 1 2 3 4 5 6 7 8 9 10 11 12 13 14 15 16 17 18 | 16 32 16 32 | Substitutions: 1 2 3 4 5 6 7 8 9 10 11 12 13 14 15 16 17 18

Comments: | Final Score | Comments:

REFEREE'S VERIFICATION		SCOREKEEPER	
FIRST REFEREE		WINNING TEAM	
SECOND REFEREE		LOSING TEAM	

KEYS:

C = Playing Captain
S = Substitution
Sx = Substitution Opponent

—| = Loss Of Rally
R = Replay
RS = Re-Serve

T = Time-Out
Tx = Time-Out Opponent
1,2,3..etc = General Point

P1, P2, P3 = Penalty Point
Px = Penalty Opponent
□ = Point Scored Off Loss Of Rally
△ = Libero Point

If the receiving team wins the rally, it receives a point which is recorded on the line of the next server's number and a square is drawn around it. Also draw a square around the same point on the team's running score. Draw a triangle around serve order position in which the Libero serves and around all points score by the Libero.

Date:	Location:		Start Time:	Finish Time:
Home Team:	Visitor Team:		Game No.:	Level:

Time-Outs		TEAM:					First Serve		Time-Outs		TEAM:	

Running Score

Serve Order	Player No.	Libero # :						1 17 1 17		Serve Order	Player No.	Libero # :	
								2 18 2 18					
I								3 19 3 19		I			
								4 20 4 20					
II								5 21 5 21		II			
								6 22 6 22					
III								7 23 7 23		III			
								8 24 8 24					
IV								9 25 9 25		IV			
								10 26 10 26					
V								11 27 11 27		V			
								12 28 12 28					
VI								13 29 13 29		VI			
								14 30 14 30					
								15 31 15 31					

Substitutions: 1 2 3 4 5 6 7 8 9 10 11 12 13 14 15 16 17 18   16 32 16 32   Substitutions: 1 2 3 4 5 6 7 8 9 10 11 12 13 14 15 16 17 18

Comments: Final Score   Comments:

REFEREE'S VERIFICATION		SCOREKEEPER	
FIRST REFEREE		WINNING TEAM	
SECOND REFEREE		LOSING TEAM	

KEYS:

C = Playing Captain   ⊣ = Loss Of Rally   T = Time-Out   P1, P2, P3 = Penalty Point

S = Substitution   R = Replay   Tx = Time-Out Opponent   Px = Penalty Opponent

Sx = Substitution Opponent   RS = Re-Serve   1,2,3..etc = General Point   ☐ = Point Scored Off Loss Of Rally

△ = Libero Point

If the receiving team wins the rally, it receives a point which is recorded on the line of the next server's number and a square is drawn around it. Also draw a square around the same point on the team's running score. Draw a triangle around serve order position in which the Libero serves and around all points score by the Libero.

Date:		Location:			Start Time:		Finish Time:	
Home Team:			Visitor Team:		Game No.:		Level:	

Time-Outs		TEAM:		First Serve		Time-Outs		TEAM:
				Running Score				

Serve Order	Player No.	Libero # :					1 17	1 17	Serve Order	Player No.	Libero # :
							2 18	2 18			
I							3 19	3 19	I		
							4 20	4 20			
II							5 21	5 21	II		
							6 22	6 22			
III							7 23	7 23	III		
							8 24	8 24			
IV							9 25	9 25	IV		
							10 26	10 26			
V							11 27	11 27	V		
							12 28	12 28			
VI							13 29	13 29	VI		
							14 30	14 30			
							15 31	15 31			

Substitutions: 1 2 3 4 5 6 7 8 9 10 11 12 13 14 15 16 17 18 | 16 32 | 16 32 | Substitutions: 1 2 3 4 5 6 7 8 9 10 11 12 13 14 15 16 17 18

Comments: | Final Score | Comments:

REFEREE'S VERIFICATION		SCOREKEEPER	
FIRST REFEREE		WINNING TEAM	
SECOND REFEREE		LOSING TEAM	

KEYS:

C = Playing Captain   ▬| = Loss Of Rally   T = Time-Out   P1, P2, P3 = Penalty Point

S = Substitution   R = Replay   Tx = Time-Out Opponent   Px = Penalty Opponent

Sx = Substitution Opponent   RS = Re-Serve   1,2,3..etc = General Point   ☐ = Point Scored Off Loss Of Rally

△ = Libero Point

If the receiving team wins the rally, it receives a point which is recorded on the line of the next server's number and a square is drawn around it. Also draw a square around the same point on the team's running score. Draw a triangle around serve order position in which the Libero serves and around all points score by the Libero.

| Date: | Location: | | Start Time: | Finish Time: |

| Home Team: | Visitor Team: | Game No.: | Level: |

| Time-Outs | | TEAM: | First Serve | Time-Outs | | TEAM: |

Running Score

Serve Order	Player No.	Libero # :								1 17 / 1 17	Serve Order	Player No.	Libero # :										

Running Score column values:
1 17 1 17
2 18 2 18
3 19 3 19
4 20 4 20
5 21 5 21
6 22 6 22
7 23 7 23
8 24 8 24
9 25 9 25
10 26 10 26
11 27 11 27
12 28 12 28
13 29 13 29
14 30 14 30
15 31 15 31
16 32 16 32

Serve Order rows: I, II, III, IV, V, VI (both left and right teams)

Final Score

| Substitutions: 1 2 3 4 5 6 7 8 9 10 11 12 13 14 15 16 17 18 | | Substitutions: 1 2 3 4 5 6 7 8 9 10 11 12 13 14 15 16 17 18 |

| Comments: | | Comments: |

REFEREE'S VERIFICATION		SCOREKEEPER	
FIRST REFEREE		WINNING TEAM	
SECOND REFEREE		LOSING TEAM	

KEYS:

C = Playing Captain
S = Substitution
Sx = Substitution Opponent

—| = Loss Of Rally
R = Replay
RS = Re-Serve

T = Time-Out
Tx = Time-Out Opponent
1,2,3..etc = General Point

P1, P2, P3 = Penalty Point
Px = Penalty Opponent
☐ = Point Scored Off Loss Of Rally
△ = Libero Point

If the receiving team wins the rally, it receives a point which is recorded on the line of the next server's number and a square is drawn around it. Also draw a square around the same point on the team's running score. Draw a triangle around serve order position in which the Libero serves and around all points score by the Libero.

| Date: | | Location: | | | | | Start Time: | | Finish Time: | |

| Home Team: | | Visitor Team: | | | Game No.: | | Level: | |

| **Time-Outs** | | TEAM: | | | **First Serve** | | **Time-Outs** | | TEAM: | |

Running Score

Serve Order	Player No.	Libero # :											Serve Order	Player No.	Libero # :											

First Serve Running Score	1	17	1	17
	2	18	2	18
	3	19	3	19
	4	20	4	20
	5	21	5	21
	6	22	6	22
	7	23	7	23
	8	24	8	24
	9	25	9	25
	10	26	10	26
	11	27	11	27
	12	28	12	28
	13	29	13	29
	14	30	14	30
	15	31	15	31
	16	32	16	32

Serve Order (left): I, II, III, IV, V, VI

Serve Order (right): I, II, III, IV, V, VI

Substitutions: 1 2 3 4 5 6 7 8 9 10 11 12 13 14 15 16 17 18 | **Substitutions:** 1 2 3 4 5 6 7 8 9 10 11 12 13 14 15 16 17 18

Comments: | Final Score | **Comments:**

REFEREE'S VERIFICATION		**SCOREKEEPER**	
FIRST REFEREE		**WINNING TEAM**	
SECOND REFEREE		**LOSING TEAM**	

KEYS:

C = Playing Captain
S = Substitution
Sx = Substitution Opponent

—| = Loss Of Rally
R = Replay
RS = Re-Serve

T = Time-Out
Tx = Time-Out Opponent
1,2,3..etc = General Point

P1, P2, P3 = Penalty Point
Px = Penalty Opponent
▢ = Point Scored Off Loss Of Rally
△ = Libero Point

If the receiving team wins the rally, it receives a point which is recorded on the line of the next server's number and a square is drawn around it. Also draw a square around the same point on the team's running score. Draw a triangle around serve order position in which the Libero serves and around all points score by the Libero.

| Date: | | Location: | | | | | | Start Time: | | Finish Time: | |

| Home Team: | | Visitor Team: | | Game No.: | | Level: |

| Time-Outs | | TEAM: | First Serve | Time-Outs | | TEAM: |
| Running Score | | | | | |

Serve Order	Player No.	Libero # :								1 17 1 17	Serve Order	Player No.	Libero # :
										2 18 2 18			
I										3 19 3 19	I		
										4 20 4 20			
II										5 21 5 21	II		
										6 22 6 22			
III										7 23 7 23	III		
										8 24 8 24			
IV										9 25 9 25	IV		
										10 26 10 26			
V										11 27 11 27	V		
										12 28 12 28			
										13 29 13 29			
VI										14 30 14 30	VI		
										15 31 15 31			

| Substitutions: 1 2 3 4 5 6 7 8 9 10 11 12 13 14 15 16 17 18 | 16 32 16 32 | Substitutions: 1 2 3 4 5 6 7 8 9 10 11 12 13 14 15 16 17 18 |
| Comments: | Final Score | Comments: |

REFEREE'S VERIFICATION		SCOREKEEPER	
FIRST REFEREE		WINNING TEAM	
SECOND REFEREE		LOSING TEAM	

KEYS:

C = Playing Captain   ⊣ = Loss Of Rally   T = Time-Out   P1, P2, P3 = Penalty Point

S = Substitution   R = Replay   Tx = Time-Out Opponent   Px = Penalty Opponent

Sx = Substitution Opponent   RS = Re-Serve   1,2,3..etc = General Point   □ = Point Scored Off Loss Of Rally

△ = Libero Point

If the receiving team wins the rally, it receives a point which is recorded on the line of the next server's number and a square is drawn around it. Also draw a square around the same point on the team's running score. Draw a triangle around serve order position in which the Libero serves and around all points score by the Libero.

Date:		Location:					Start Time:		Finish Time:	
Home Team:			Visitor Team:				Game No.:		Level:	

Time-Outs		TEAM:			First Serve		Time-Outs		TEAM:	

			Running Score		

Serve Order	Player No.	Libero # :							1	17	1	17	Serve Order	Player No.	Libero # :
I									2	18	2	18	I		
									3	19	3	19			
									4	20	4	20			
II									5	21	5	21	II		
									6	22	6	22			
III									7	23	7	23	III		
									8	24	8	24			
IV									9	25	9	25	IV		
									10	26	10	26			
V									11	27	11	27	V		
									12	28	12	28			
									13	29	13	29			
VI									14	30	14	30	VI		
									15	31	15	31			

Substitutions: 1 2 3 4 5 6 7 8 9 10 11 12 13 14 15 16 17 18 | 16 | 32 | 16 | 32 | Substitutions: 1 2 3 4 5 6 7 8 9 10 11 12 13 14 15 16 17 18

Comments: | Final Score | | Comments:

REFEREE'S VERIFICATION		SCOREKEEPER	
FIRST REFEREE		WINNING TEAM	
SECOND REFEREE		LOSING TEAM	

KEYS:

C = Playing Captain
S = Substitution
Sx = Substitution Opponent

—| = Loss Of Rally
R = Replay
RS = Re-Serve

T = Time-Out
Tx = Time-Out Opponent
1,2,3..etc = General Point

P1, P2, P3 = Penalty Point
Px = Penalty Opponent
☐ = Point Scored Off Loss Of Rally
△ = Libero Point

If the receiving team wins the rally, it receives a point which is recorded on the line of the next server's number and a square is drawn around it. Also draw a square around the same point on the team's running score. Draw a triangle around serve order position in which the Libero serves and around all points score by the Libero.

Date:	Location:		Start Time:	Finish Time:
Home Team:	Visitor Team:		Game No.:	Level:

Time-Outs		TEAM:	First Serve	Time-Outs		TEAM:
			Running Score			

Serve Order	Player No.	Libero # :											Running Score				Serve Order	Player No.	Libero # :											
I													1 17 2 18	1 17 2 18		I														
													3 19 4 20	3 19 4 20																
II													5 21 6 22	5 21 6 22		II														
III													7 23 8 24	7 23 8 24		III														
IV													9 25 10 26	9 25 10 26		IV														
V													11 27 12 28	11 27 12 28		V														
													13 29	13 29																
VI													14 30 15 31	14 30 15 31		VI														

Substitutions: 1 2 3 4 5 6 7 8 9 10 11 12 13 14 15 16 17 18 | 16 32 | 16 32 | Substitutions: 1 2 3 4 5 6 7 8 9 10 11 12 13 14 15 16 17 18

Comments: | Final Score | Comments:

REFEREE'S VERIFICATION		SCOREKEEPER	
FIRST REFEREE		WINNING TEAM	
SECOND REFEREE		LOSING TEAM	

KEYS:

C = Playing Captain
S = Substitution
Sx = Substitution Opponent

—| = Loss Of Rally
R = Replay
RS = Re-Serve

T = Time-Out
Tx = Time-Out Opponent
1,2,3..etc = General Point

P1, P2, P3 = Penalty Point
Px = Penalty Opponent
☐ = Point Scored Off Loss Of Rally
△ = Libero Point

If the receiving team wins the rally, it receives a point which is recorded on the line of the next server's number and a square is drawn around it. Also draw a square around the same point on the team's running score. Draw a triangle around serve order position in which the Libero serves and around all points score by the Libero.

Date:		Location:				Start Time:		Finish Time:	
Home Team:			Visitor Team:			Game No.:		Level:	

Time-Outs		TEAM:								First Serve				Time-Outs		TEAM:								
										Running Score															

TEAM (left):

Serve Order	Player No.	Libero # :									1 17	1 17	Serve Order	Player No.	Libero # :
											2 18	2 18			
I		--------									3 19	3 19	I		--------
											4 20	4 20			
II		--------									5 21	5 21	II		--------
											6 22	6 22			
III		--------									7 23	7 23	III		--------
											8 24	8 24			
IV		--------									9 25	9 25	IV		--------
											10 26	10 26			
V		--------									11 27	11 27	V		--------
											12 28	12 28			
											13 29	13 29			
VI		--------									14 30	14 30	VI		--------
											15 31	15 31			

Substitutions: 1 2 3 4 5 6 7 8 9 10 11 12 13 14 15 16 17 18 | 16 32 | 16 32 | **Substitutions:** 1 2 3 4 5 6 7 8 9 10 11 12 13 14 15 16 17 18

Comments: | Final Score | **Comments:**

REFEREE'S VERIFICATION		SCOREKEEPER	
FIRST REFEREE		WINNING TEAM	
SECOND REFEREE		LOSING TEAM	

KEYS:

C = Playing Captain
S = Substitution
Sx = Substitution Opponent

—| = Loss Of Rally
R = Replay
RS = Re-Serve

T = Time-Out
Tx = Time-Out Opponent
1,2,3..etc = General Point

P1, P2, P3 = Penalty Point
Px = Penalty Opponent
☐ = Point Scored Off Loss Of Rally
△ = Libero Point

If the receiving team wins the rally, it receives a point which is recorded on the line of the next server's number and a square is drawn around it. Also draw a square around the same point on the team's running score. Draw a triangle around serve order position in which the Libero serves and around all points score by the Libero.

| Date: | Location: | | Start Time: | Finish Time: |

Home Team: Visitor Team: Game No.:   Level:

Time-Outs		TEAM:	First Serve	Time-Outs		TEAM:

Running Score

Serve Order	Player No.	Libero # :		Serve Order	Player No.	Libero # :

Running Score values:

1 | 17   1 | 17
2 | 18   2 | 18
3 | 19   3 | 19
4 | 20   4 | 20
5 | 21   5 | 21
6 | 22   6 | 22
7 | 23   7 | 23
8 | 24   8 | 24
9 | 25   9 | 25
10 | 26   10 | 26
11 | 27   11 | 27
12 | 28   12 | 28
13 | 29   13 | 29
14 | 30   14 | 30
15 | 31   15 | 31
16 | 32   16 | 32

Serve Order rows: I, II, III, IV, V, VI

Substitutions: 1 2 3 4 5 6 7 8 9 10 11 12 13 14 15 16 17 18   Substitutions: 1 2 3 4 5 6 7 8 9 10 11 12 13 14 15 16 17 18

Comments: Final Score   Comments:

REFEREE'S VERIFICATION		SCOREKEEPER	
FIRST REFEREE		WINNING TEAM	
SECOND REFEREE		LOSING TEAM	

KEYS:

C = Playing Captain
S = Substitution
Sx = Substitution Opponent

⊣ = Loss Of Rally
R = Replay
RS = Re-Serve

T = Time-Out
Tx = Time-Out Opponent
1,2,3..etc = General Point

P1, P2, P3 = Penalty Point
Px = Penalty Opponent
☐ = Point Scored Off Loss Of Rally
△ = Libero Point

If the receiving team wins the rally, it receives a point which is recorded on the line of the next server's number and a square is drawn around it. Also draw a square around the same point on the team's running score. Draw a triangle around serve order position in which the Libero serves and around all points score by the Libero.

Date:		Location:						Start Time:		Finish Time:	

Home Team:			Visitor Team:					Game No.:		Level:	

Time-Outs		TEAM:		First Serve		Time-Outs		TEAM:	

| | | | | Running Score | | | | | |

| Serve Order | Player No. | Libero # : | | 1 17 1 17 | Serve Order | Player No. | Libero # : | |

Running Score (center column):

1	17	1	17
2	18	2	18
3	19	3	19
4	20	4	20
5	21	5	21
6	22	6	22
7	23	7	23
8	24	8	24
9	25	9	25
10	26	10	26
11	27	11	27
12	28	12	28
13	29	13	29
14	30	14	30
15	31	15	31
16	32	16	32

Serve Order positions: I, II, III, IV, V, VI (both left and right teams)

Substitutions:1 2 3 4 5 6 7 8 9 10 11 12 13 14 15 16 17 18

Final Score

Substitutions:1 2 3 4 5 6 7 8 9 10 11 12 13 14 15 16 17 18

Comments: | | Comments:

REFEREE'S VERIFICATION		SCOREKEEPER	
FIRST REFEREE		WINNING TEAM	
SECOND REFEREE		LOSING TEAM	

KEYS:

C = Playing Captain   —| = Loss Of Rally   T = Time-Out   P1, P2, P3 = Penalty Point

S = Substitution   R = Replay   Tx = Time-Out Opponent   Px = Penalty Opponent

Sx = Substitution Opponent   RS = Re-Serve   1,2,3..etc = General Point   □ = Point Scored Off Loss Of Rally

△ = Libero Point

If the receiving team wins the rally, it receives a point which is recorded on the line of the next server's number and a square is drawn around it. Also draw a square around the same point on the team's running score. Draw a triangle around serve order position in which the Libero serves and around all points score by the Libero.

Date:	Location:			Start Time:	Finish Time:

Home Team: Visitor Team: Game No.:   Level:

Time-Outs		TEAM:						First Serve		Time-Outs		TEAM:	

Running Score

Serve Order	Player No.	Libero # :						1 · 17	1 · 17	Serve Order	Player No.	Libero # :	
								2 · 18	2 · 18				
I								3 · 19	3 · 19	I			
								4 · 20	4 · 20				
II								5 · 21	5 · 21	II			
								6 · 22	6 · 22				
III								7 · 23	7 · 23	III			
								8 · 24	8 · 24				
IV								9 · 25	9 · 25	IV			
								10 · 26	10 · 26				
V								11 · 27	11 · 27	V			
								12 · 28	12 · 28				
VI								13 · 29	13 · 29	VI			
								14 · 30	14 · 30				
								15 · 31	15 · 31				

Substitutions: 1 2 3 4 5 6 7 8 9 10 11 12 13 14 15 16 17 18   16 · 32   16 · 32   Substitutions: 1 2 3 4 5 6 7 8 9 10 11 12 13 14 15 16 17 18

Comments: Final Score   Comments:

REFEREE'S VERIFICATION		SCOREKEEPER	
FIRST REFEREE		WINNING TEAM	
SECOND REFEREE		LOSING TEAM	

KEYS:

C = Playing Captain   ⊣ = Loss Of Rally   T = Time-Out   P1, P2, P3 = Penalty Point

S = Substitution   R = Replay   Tx = Time-Out Opponent   Px = Penalty Opponent

Sx = Substitution Opponent   RS = Re-Serve   1,2,3..etc = General Point   □ = Point Scored Off Loss Of Rally

△ = Libero Point

If the receiving team wins the rally, it receives a point which is recorded on the line of the next server's number and a square is drawn around it. Also draw a square around the same point on the team's running score. Draw a triangle around serve order position in which the Libero serves and around all points score by the Libero.

Date:		Location:							Start Time:		Finish Time:		
Home Team:			Visitor Team:						Game No.:		Level:		

| Time-Outs | | TEAM: | | | | | | | | First Serve | | Time-Outs | | TEAM: | | | | | | | | |

Running Score

Serve Order	Player No.	Libero # :								1 17 1 17	2 18 2 18	Serve Order	Player No.	Libero # :									
I										3 19 3 19	4 20 4 20	I											
II										5 21 5 21	6 22 6 22	II											
III										7 23 7 23	8 24 8 24	III											
IV										9 25 9 25	10 26 10 26	IV											
V										11 27 11 27	12 28 12 28	V											
VI										13 29 13 29	14 30 14 30	VI											
										15 31 15 31													

Substitutions: 1 2 3 4 5 6 7 8 9 10 11 12 13 14 15 16 17 18

| | | | | | 16 32 16 32 | Substitutions: 1 2 3 4 5 6 7 8 9 10 11 12 13 14 15 16 17 18 |

Comments:

Final Score

Comments:

REFEREE'S VERIFICATION		SCOREKEEPER	
FIRST REFEREE		WINNING TEAM	
SECOND REFEREE		LOSING TEAM	

KEYS:

C = Playing Captain   ▬| = Loss Of Rally   T = Time-Out   P1, P2, P3 = Penalty Point
S = Substitution   R = Replay   Tx = Time-Out Opponent   Px = Penalty Opponent
Sx = Substitution Opponent   RS = Re-Serve   1,2,3..etc = General Point   ☐ = Point Scored Off Loss Of Rally
△ = Libero Point

If the receiving team wins the rally, it receives a point which is recorded on the line of the next server's number and a square is drawn around it. Also draw a square around the same point on the team's running score. Draw a triangle around serve order position in which the Libero serves and around all points score by the Libero.

| Date: | | Location: | | | Start Time: | | Finish Time: | |
| Home Team: | | | Visitor Team: | | Game No.: | | Level: | |

Time-Outs		TEAM:					First Serve		Time-Outs		TEAM:		
							Running Score						

Serve Order	Player No.	Libero # :						1 17 1 17 2 18 2 18		Serve Order	Player No.	Libero # :			
I								3 19 3 19 4 20 4 20		I					
II								5 21 5 21 6 22 6 22		II					
III								7 23 7 23 8 24 8 24		III					
IV								9 25 9 25 10 26 10 26		IV					
V								11 27 11 27 12 28 12 28 13 29 13 29		V					
VI								14 30 14 30 15 31 15 31		VI					

Substitutions: 1 2 3 4 5 6 7 8 9 10 11 12 13 14 15 16 17 18	16 32 16 32	Substitutions: 1 2 3 4 5 6 7 8 9 10 11 12 13 14 15 16 17 18
Comments:	Final Score	Comments:

REFEREE'S VERIFICATION		SCOREKEEPER	
FIRST REFEREE		WINNING TEAM	
SECOND REFEREE		LOSING TEAM	

KEYS:

C = Playing Captain
S = Substitution
Sx = Substitution Opponent

—| = Loss Of Rally
R = Replay
RS = Re-Serve

T = Time-Out
Tx = Time-Out Opponent
1,2,3..etc = General Point

P1, P2, P3 = Penalty Point
Px = Penalty Opponent
☐ = Point Scored Off Loss Of Rally
△ = Libero Point

If the receiving team wins the rally, it receives a point which is recorded on the line of the next server's number and a square is drawn around it. Also draw a square around the same point on the team's running score. Draw a triangle around serve order position in which the Libero serves and around all points score by the Libero.

| Date: | | Location: | | | | | | Start Time: | | Finish Time: | |
| Home Team: | | | Visitor Team: | | | | | Game No.: | | Level: | |

Time-Outs		TEAM:		First Serve		Time-Outs		TEAM:	

Running Score

Serve Order	Player No.	Libero # :			First Serve Running Score		Serve Order	Player No.	Libero # :
I					1 17 1 17 / 2 18 2 18		I		
II					3 19 3 19 / 4 20 4 20 / 5 21 5 21 / 6 22 6 22		II		
III					7 23 7 23 / 8 24 8 24		III		
IV					9 25 9 25 / 10 26 10 26		IV		
V					11 27 11 27 / 12 28 12 28 / 13 29 13 29		V		
VI					14 30 14 30 / 15 31 15 31		VI		

Substitutions: 1 2 3 4 5 6 7 8 9 10 11 12 13 14 15 16 17 18 | 16 32 16 32 | Substitutions: 1 2 3 4 5 6 7 8 9 10 11 12 13 14 15 16 17 18

Comments: | Final Score | Comments:

REFEREE'S VERIFICATION		SCOREKEEPER	
FIRST REFEREE		WINNING TEAM	
SECOND REFEREE		LOSING TEAM	

KEYS:

C = Playing Captain   ⊣ = Loss Of Rally   T = Time-Out   P1, P2, P3 = Penalty Point
S = Substitution   R = Replay   Tx = Time-Out Opponent   Px = Penalty Opponent
Sx = Substitution Opponent   RS = Re-Serve   1,2,3..etc = General Point   ☐ = Point Scored Off Loss Of Rally
△ = Libero Point

If the receiving team wins the rally, it receives a point which is recorded on the line of the next server's number and a square is drawn around it. Also draw a square around the same point on the team's running score. Draw a triangle around serve order position in which the Libero serves and around all points score by the Libero.

Date:	Location:		Start Time:	Finish Time:
Home Team:	Visitor Team:		Game No.:	Level:

Time-Outs		TEAM:		First Serve	Time-Outs		TEAM:

Running Score

Serve Order	Player No.	Libero # :												Running Score	Serve Order	Player No.	Libero # :										

Running Score columns:
1 17 1 17
2 18 2 18
3 19 3 19
4 20 4 20
5 21 5 21
6 22 6 22
7 23 7 23
8 24 8 24
9 25 9 25
10 26 10 26
11 27 11 27
12 28 12 28
13 29 13 29
14 30 14 30
15 31 15 31
16 32 16 32

Serve Order rows (both teams): I, II, III, IV, V, VI

Substitutions:1 2 3 4 5 6 7 8 9 10 11 12 13 14 15 16 17 18   Substitutions:1 2 3 4 5 6 7 8 9 10 11 12 13 14 15 16 17 18

Comments:

Final Score

Comments:

REFEREE'S VERIFICATION		SCOREKEEPER	
FIRST REFEREE		WINNING TEAM	
SECOND REFEREE		LOSING TEAM	

KEYS:

C = Playing Captain
S = Substitution
Sx = Substitution Opponent

—| = Loss Of Rally
R = Replay
RS = Re-Serve

T = Time-Out
Tx = Time-Out Opponent
1,2,3..etc = General Point

P1, P2, P3 = Penalty Point
Px = Penalty Opponent
☐ = Point Scored Off Loss Of Rally
△ = Libero Point

If the receiving team wins the rally, it receives a point which is recorded on the line of the next server's number and a square is drawn around it. Also draw a square around the same point on the team's running score. Draw a triangle around serve order position in which the Libero serves and around all points score by the Libero.

Date:	Location:		Start Time:	Finish Time:
Home Team:	Visitor Team:		Game No.:	Level:

Time-Outs		TEAM:	First Serve	Time-Outs		TEAM:

Running Score

Serve Order	Player No.	Libero # :											1 17 1 17	Serve Order	Player No.	Libero # :
													2 18 2 18			
I													3 19 3 19	I		
													4 20 4 20			
II													5 21 5 21	II		
													6 22 6 22			
III													7 23 7 23	III		
													8 24 8 24			
IV													9 25 9 25	IV		
													10 26 10 26			
V													11 27 11 27	V		
													12 28 12 28			
VI													13 29 13 29	VI		
													14 30 14 30			
													15 31 15 31			

Substitutions: 1 2 3 4 5 6 7 8 9 10 11 12 13 14 15 16 17 18 | 16 32 16 32 | Substitutions: 1 2 3 4 5 6 7 8 9 10 11 12 13 14 15 16 17 18

Comments: | Final Score | Comments:

REFEREE'S VERIFICATION		SCOREKEEPER	
FIRST REFEREE		WINNING TEAM	
SECOND REFEREE		LOSING TEAM	

KEYS:

C = Playing Captain
S = Substitution
Sx = Substitution Opponent

— | = Loss Of Rally
R = Replay
RS = Re-Serve

T = Time-Out
Tx = Time-Out Opponent
1,2,3..etc = General Point

P1, P2, P3 = Penalty Point
Px = Penalty Opponent
☐ = Point Scored Off Loss Of Rally
△ = Libero Point

If the receiving team wins the rally, it receives a point which is recorded on the line of the next server's number and a square is drawn around it. Also draw a square around the same point on the team's running score. Draw a triangle around serve order position in which the Libero serves and around all points score by the Libero.

| Date: | | Location: | | | | Start Time: | | Finish Time: | |

| Home Team: | | Visitor Team: | | | Game No.: | | Level: | |

<table>
<tr><td colspan="2">Time-Outs</td><td rowspan="2">TEAM:</td><td rowspan="2"></td><td rowspan="2" colspan="2">First
Serve</td><td colspan="2">Time-Outs</td><td rowspan="2">TEAM:</td><td rowspan="2"></td></tr>
<tr><td></td><td></td><td></td><td></td></tr>
<tr><td>Serve
Order</td><td>Player No.</td><td colspan="2">Libero # :</td><td colspan="2">Running Score</td><td>Serve
Order</td><td>Player No.</td><td colspan="2">Libero # :</td></tr>
<tr><td>I</td><td></td><td></td><td></td><td>1 ¦ 17
2 ¦ 18</td><td>1 ¦ 17
2 ¦ 18</td><td>I</td><td></td><td></td><td></td></tr>
<tr><td>II</td><td></td><td></td><td></td><td>3 ¦ 19
4 ¦ 20
5 ¦ 21
6 ¦ 22</td><td>3 ¦ 19
4 ¦ 20
5 ¦ 21
6 ¦ 22</td><td>II</td><td></td><td></td><td></td></tr>
<tr><td>III</td><td></td><td></td><td></td><td>7 ¦ 23
8 ¦ 24</td><td>7 ¦ 23
8 ¦ 24</td><td>III</td><td></td><td></td><td></td></tr>
<tr><td>IV</td><td></td><td></td><td></td><td>9 ¦ 25
10 ¦ 26</td><td>9 ¦ 25
10 ¦ 26</td><td>IV</td><td></td><td></td><td></td></tr>
<tr><td>V</td><td></td><td></td><td></td><td>11 ¦ 27
12 ¦ 28
13 ¦ 29</td><td>11 ¦ 27
12 ¦ 28
13 ¦ 29</td><td>V</td><td></td><td></td><td></td></tr>
<tr><td>VI</td><td></td><td></td><td></td><td>14 ¦ 30
15 ¦ 31</td><td>14 ¦ 30
15 ¦ 31</td><td>VI</td><td></td><td></td><td></td></tr>
</table>

Substitutions: 1 2 3 4 5 6 7 8 9 10 11 12 13 14 15 16 17 18 | 16 ¦ 32 | 16 ¦ 32 | Substitutions: 1 2 3 4 5 6 7 8 9 10 11 12 13 14 15 16 17 18

Comments: | Final Score | Comments:

REFEREE'S VERIFICATION		SCOREKEEPER	
FIRST REFEREE		WINNING TEAM	
SECOND REFEREE		LOSING TEAM	

KEYS:

C = Playing Captain
S = Substitution
Sx = Substitution Opponent

–| = Loss Of Rally
R = Replay
RS = Re-Serve

T = Time-Out
Tx = Time-Out Opponent
1,2,3..etc = General Point

P1, P2, P3 = Penalty Point
Px = Penalty Opponent
☐ = Point Scored Off Loss Of Rally
△ = Libero Point

If the receiving team wins the rally, it receives a point which is recorded on the line of the next server's number and a square is drawn around it. Also draw a square around the same point on the team's running score. Draw a triangle around serve order position in which the Libero serves and around all points score by the Libero.

| Date: | | Location: | | | | Start Time: | | Finish Time: | |

| Home Team: | | Visitor Team: | | | Game No.: | | Level: | |

Scoresheet

Time-Outs		TEAM:	First Serve		Time-Outs		TEAM:
			Running Score				

Serve Order	Player No.	Libero # :										1 17	1 17	Serve Order	Player No.	Libero # :								
											2 18	2 18											
I											3 19	3 19	I										
											4 20	4 20											
II											5 21	5 21	II										
											6 22	6 22											
III											7 23	7 23	III										
											8 24	8 24											
IV											9 25	9 25	IV										
											10 26	10 26											
V											11 27	11 27	V										
											12 28	12 28											
											13 29	13 29											
VI											14 30	14 30	VI										
											15 31	15 31											

Substitutions: 1 2 3 4 5 6 7 8 9 10 11 12 13 14 15 16 17 18	16 32	16 32	Substitutions: 1 2 3 4 5 6 7 8 9 10 11 12 13 14 15 16 17 18
Comments:	Final Score		Comments:

REFEREE'S VERIFICATION		SCOREKEEPER	
FIRST REFEREE		WINNING TEAM	
SECOND REFEREE		LOSING TEAM	

KEYS:

C = Playing Captain ▬| = Loss Of Rally T = Time-Out P1, P2, P3 = Penalty Point
S = Substitution R = Replay Tx = Time-Out Opponent Px = Penalty Opponent
Sx = Substitution Opponent RS = Re-Serve 1,2,3..etc = General Point ☐ = Point Scored Off Loss Of Rally
△ = Libero Point

If the receiving team wins the rally, it receives a point which is recorded on the line of the next server's number and a square is drawn around it. Also draw a square around the same point on the team's running score. Draw a triangle around serve order position in which the Libero serves and around all points score by the Libero.

Date:	Location:		Start Time:	Finish Time:

Home Team:	Visitor Team:	Game No.:	Level:

Time-Outs TEAM:

First Serve

Time-Outs TEAM:

Serve Order	Player No.	Libero # :	First Serve Running Score	Serve Order	Player No.	Libero # :
I			1 ¦ 17 1 ¦ 17	I		
			2 ¦ 18 2 ¦ 18			
II			3 ¦ 19 3 ¦ 19	II		
			4 ¦ 20 4 ¦ 20			
III			5 ¦ 21 5 ¦ 21	III		
			6 ¦ 22 6 ¦ 22			
IV			7 ¦ 23 7 ¦ 23	IV		
			8 ¦ 24 8 ¦ 24			
V			9 ¦ 25 9 ¦ 25	V		
			10 ¦ 26 10 ¦ 26			
VI			11 ¦ 27 11 ¦ 27	VI		
			12 ¦ 28 12 ¦ 28			
			13 ¦ 29 13 ¦ 29			
			14 ¦ 30 14 ¦ 30			
			15 ¦ 31 15 ¦ 31			

Substitutions: 1 2 3 4 5 6 7 8 9 10 11 12 13 14 15 16 17 18

16 ¦ 32   16 ¦ 32

Substitutions: 1 2 3 4 5 6 7 8 9 10 11 12 13 14 15 16 17 18

Comments:

Final Score

Comments:

REFEREE'S VERIFICATION		**SCOREKEEPER**	
FIRST REFEREE		**WINNING TEAM**	
SECOND REFEREE		**LOSING TEAM**	

KEYS:

C = Playing Captain
S = Substitution
Sx = Substitution Opponent

━| = Loss Of Rally
R = Replay
RS = Re-Serve

T = Time-Out
Tx = Time-Out Opponent
1,2,3..etc = General Point

P1, P2, P3 = Penalty Point
Px = Penalty Opponent
☐ = Point Scored Off Loss Of Rally
△ = Libero Point

If the receiving team wins the rally, it receives a point which is recorded on the line of the next server's number and a square is drawn around it. Also draw a square around the same point on the team's running score. Draw a triangle around serve order position in which the Libero serves and around all points score by the Libero.

Date:	Location:		Start Time:	Finish Time:
Home Team:	Visitor Team:		Game No.:	Level:

Time-Outs		TEAM:		First Serve	Time-Outs		TEAM:	

Running Score

| Serve Order | Player No. | Libero # : | | 1 : 17 | 1 : 17 | Serve Order | Player No. | Libero # : |

| | | | | 2 : 18 | 2 : 18 | | | |

I — 3 : 19 | 3 : 19 — **I**
4 : 20 | 4 : 20

II — 5 : 21 | 5 : 21 — **II**
6 : 22 | 6 : 22

III — 7 : 23 | 7 : 23 — **III**
8 : 24 | 8 : 24

IV — 9 : 25 | 9 : 25 — **IV**
10 : 26 | 10 : 26

V — 11 : 27 | 11 : 27 — **V**
12 : 28 | 12 : 28

VI — 13 : 29 | 13 : 29 — **VI**
14 : 30 | 14 : 30
15 : 31 | 15 : 31

Substitutions: 1 2 3 4 5 6 7 8 9 10 11 12 13 14 15 16 17 18   16 : 32 | 16 : 32   Substitutions: 1 2 3 4 5 6 7 8 9 10 11 12 13 14 15 16 17 18

Comments: Final Score   Comments:

REFEREE'S VERIFICATION		SCOREKEEPER	
FIRST REFEREE		WINNING TEAM	
SECOND REFEREE		LOSING TEAM	

KEYS:

C = Playing Captain   ⊣ = Loss Of Rally   T = Time-Out   P1, P2, P3 = Penalty Point

S = Substitution   R = Replay   Tx = Time-Out Opponent   Px = Penalty Opponent

Sx = Substitution Opponent   RS = Re-Serve   1,2,3..etc = General Point   ☐ = Point Scored Off Loss Of Rally

△ = Libero Point

If the receiving team wins the rally, it receives a point which is recorded on the line of the next server's number and a square is drawn around it. Also draw a square around the same point on the team's running score. Draw a triangle around serve order position in which the Libero serves and around all points score by the Libero.

Date:	Location:		Start Time:	Finish Time:

Home Team:	Visitor Team:	Game No.:	Level:

Time-Outs	TEAM:	First Serve	Time-Outs	TEAM:

Running Score

Serve Order	Player No.	Libero # :								1	17	1	17	Serve Order	Player No.	Libero # :
										2	18	2	18			
I										3	19	3	19	I		
										4	20	4	20			
II										5	21	5	21	II		
										6	22	6	22			
III										7	23	7	23	III		
										8	24	8	24			
IV										9	25	9	25	IV		
										10	26	10	26			
V										11	27	11	27	V		
										12	28	12	28			
										13	29	13	29			
VI										14	30	14	30	VI		
										15	31	15	31			

Substitutions: 1 2 3 4 5 6 7 8 9 10 11 12 13 14 15 16 17 18 | 16 | 32 | 16 | 32 | **Substitutions:** 1 2 3 4 5 6 7 8 9 10 11 12 13 14 15 16 17 18

Comments: | **Final Score** | **Comments:**

REFEREE'S VERIFICATION		SCOREKEEPER	
FIRST REFEREE		WINNING TEAM	
SECOND REFEREE		LOSING TEAM	

KEYS:

C = Playing Captain
S = Substitution
Sx = Substitution Opponent

⊣ = Loss Of Rally
R = Replay
RS = Re-Serve

T = Time-Out
Tx = Time-Out Opponent
1,2,3..etc = General Point

P1, P2, P3 = Penalty Point
Px = Penalty Opponent
☐ = Point Scored Off Loss Of Rally
△ = Libero Point

If the receiving team wins the rally, it receives a point which is recorded on the line of the next server's number and a square is drawn around it. Also draw a square around the same point on the team's running score. Draw a triangle around serve order position in which the Libero serves and around all points score by the Libero.

Date:	Location:				Start Time:	Finish Time:	
Home Team:		Visitor Team:			Game No.:	Level:	

Time-Outs		TEAM:			First Serve	Time-Outs		TEAM:

Running Score

Serve Order	Player No.	Libero # :					Running Score			Serve Order	Player No.	Libero # :
I							1 17	1 17		I		
							2 18	2 18				
II							3 19	3 19		II		
							4 20	4 20				
							5 21	5 21				
III							6 22	6 22		III		
							7 23	7 23				
							8 24	8 24				
IV							9 25	9 25		IV		
							10 26	10 26				
V							11 27	11 27		V		
							12 28	12 28				
							13 29	13 29				
VI							14 30	14 30		VI		
							15 31	15 31				

Substitutions: 1 2 3 4 5 6 7 8 9 10 11 12 13 14 15 16 17 18 | 16 32 | 16 32 | Substitutions: 1 2 3 4 5 6 7 8 9 10 11 12 13 14 15 16 17 18

Comments: | Final Score | Comments:

REFEREE'S VERIFICATION		SCOREKEEPER	
FIRST REFEREE		WINNING TEAM	
SECOND REFEREE		LOSING TEAM	

KEYS:

C = Playing Captain
S = Substitution
Sx = Substitution Opponent

▬| = Loss Of Rally
R = Replay
RS = Re-Serve

T = Time-Out
Tx = Time-Out Opponent
1,2,3..etc = General Point

P1, P2, P3 = Penalty Point
Px = Penalty Opponent
☐ = Point Scored Off Loss Of Rally
△ = Libero Point

If the receiving team wins the rally, it receives a point which is recorded on the line of the next server's number and a square is drawn around it. Also draw a square around the same point on the team's running score. Draw a triangle around serve order position in which the Libero serves and around all points score by the Libero.

Date:	Location:		Start Time:	Finish Time:
Home Team:	Visitor Team:		Game No.:	Level:

Time-Outs		TEAM:		First Serve	Time-Outs		TEAM:	
				Running Score				

Serve Order	Player No.	Libero # :														Running Score		Serve Order	Player No.	Libero # :															
I															1 17 1 17			I															
															2 18 2 18																		
II															3 19 3 19			II															
															4 20 4 20																		
III															5 21 5 21			III															
															6 22 6 22																		
IV															7 23 7 23			IV															
															8 24 8 24																		
V															9 25 9 25			V															
															10 26 10 26																		
VI															11 27 11 27			VI															
															12 28 12 28																		
															13 29 13 29																		
															14 30 14 30																		
															15 31 15 31																		

Substitutions: 1 2 3 4 5 6 7 8 9 10 11 12 13 14 15 16 17 18 | 16 32 16 32 | **Substitutions:** 1 2 3 4 5 6 7 8 9 10 11 12 13 14 15 16 17 18

Comments: | Final Score | **Comments:**

REFEREE'S VERIFICATION		SCOREKEEPER	
FIRST REFEREE		WINNING TEAM	
SECOND REFEREE		LOSING TEAM	

KEYS:

C = Playing Captain ⊣ = Loss Of Rally T = Time-Out P1, P2, P3 = Penalty Point

S = Substitution R = Replay Tx = Time-Out Opponent Px = Penalty Opponent

Sx = Substitution Opponent RS = Re-Serve 1,2,3..etc = General Point ☐ = Point Scored Off Loss Of Rally

△ = Libero Point

If the receiving team wins the rally, it receives a point which is recorded on the line of the next server's number and a square is drawn around it. Also draw a square around the same point on the team's running score. Draw a triangle around serve order position in which the Libero serves and around all points score by the Libero.

Date:		Location:				Start Time:		Finish Time:	
Home Team:			Visitor Team:			Game No.:		Level:	

Time-Outs		TEAM:		First Serve	Time-Outs		TEAM:	

Running Score

Serve Order	Player No.	Libero # :											Running Score		Serve Order	Player No.	Libero # :										
I													1 17	1 17	I												
													2 18	2 18													
II													3 19	3 19	II												
													4 20	4 20													
III													5 21	5 21	III												
													6 22	6 22													
IV													7 23	7 23	IV												
													8 24	8 24													
V													9 25	9 25	V												
													10 26	10 26													
VI													11 27	11 27	VI												
													12 28	12 28													
													13 29	13 29													
													14 30	14 30													
													15 31	15 31													

Substitutions: 1 2 3 4 5 6 7 8 9 10 11 12 13 14 15 16 17 18 | 16 32 | 16 32 | **Substitutions:** 1 2 3 4 5 6 7 8 9 10 11 12 13 14 15 16 17 18

Comments:

Final Score

Comments:

REFEREE'S VERIFICATION		SCOREKEEPER	
FIRST REFEREE		WINNING TEAM	
SECOND REFEREE		LOSING TEAM	

KEYS:

C = Playing Captain   —| = Loss Of Rally   T = Time-Out   P1, P2, P3 = Penalty Point
S = Substitution   R = Replay   Tx = Time-Out Opponent Px = Penalty Opponent
Sx = Substitution Opponent RS = Re-Serve   1,2,3..etc = General Point   ☐ = Point Scored Off Loss Of Rally
                                                                            △ = Libero Point

If the receiving team wins the rally, it receives a point which is recorded on the line of the next server's number and a square is drawn around it. Also draw a square around the same point on the team's running score. Draw a triangle around serve order position in which the Libero serves and around all points score by the Libero.

Date:	Location:		Start Time:	Finish Time:

Home Team:	Visitor Team:	Game No.:	Level:

Time-Outs		TEAM:			First Serve		Time-Outs		TEAM:
					Running Score				

Serve Order	Player No.	Libero # :								1 ¦ 17	1 ¦ 17	Serve Order	Player No.	Libero # :							
										2 ¦ 18	2 ¦ 18										
I										3 ¦ 19	3 ¦ 19	I									
										4 ¦ 20	4 ¦ 20										
II										5 ¦ 21	5 ¦ 21	II									
										6 ¦ 22	6 ¦ 22										
III										7 ¦ 23	7 ¦ 23	III									
										8 ¦ 24	8 ¦ 24										
IV										9 ¦ 25	9 ¦ 25	IV									
										10 ¦ 26	10 ¦ 26										
V										11 ¦ 27	11 ¦ 27	V									
										12 ¦ 28	12 ¦ 28										
										13 ¦ 29	13 ¦ 29										
VI										14 ¦ 30	14 ¦ 30	VI									
										15 ¦ 31	15 ¦ 31										

Substitutions: 1 2 3 4 5 6 7 8 9 10 11 12 13 14 15 16 17 18 | 16 ¦ 32 | 16 ¦ 32 | Substitutions: 1 2 3 4 5 6 7 8 9 10 11 12 13 14 15 16 17 18

Comments: | Final Score | Comments:

REFEREE'S VERIFICATION		SCOREKEEPER	
FIRST REFEREE		WINNING TEAM	
SECOND REFEREE		LOSING TEAM	

KEYS:

C = Playing Captain
S = Substitution
Sx = Substitution Opponent

—| = Loss Of Rally
R = Replay
RS = Re-Serve

T = Time-Out
Tx = Time-Out Opponent
1,2,3..etc = General Point

P1, P2, P3 = Penalty Point
Px = Penalty Opponent
☐ = Point Scored Off Loss Of Rally
△ = Libero Point

If the receiving team wins the rally, it receives a point which is recorded on the line of the next server's number and a square is drawn around it. Also draw a square around the same point on the team's running score. Draw a triangle around serve order position in which the Libero serves and around all points score by the Libero.

| Date: | | Location: | | | | | Start Time: | | Finish Time: | |

| Home Team: | | Visitor Team: | | | | Game No.: | | Level: | |

| Time-Outs | | TEAM: | | | First Serve | | Time-Outs | | TEAM: | |

<table>
<tr><td colspan="2">Time-Outs</td><td rowspan="2">TEAM:</td><td colspan="2">First
Serve</td><td colspan="2">Time-Outs</td><td rowspan="2">TEAM:</td></tr>
<tr><td></td><td></td><td colspan="2">Running Score</td><td></td><td></td></tr>
<tr><td>Serve Order</td><td>Player No.</td><td>Libero # :</td><td>1 ¦17 2 ¦18</td><td>1 ¦17 2 ¦18</td><td>Serve Order</td><td>Player No.</td><td>Libero # :</td></tr>
<tr><td>I</td><td></td><td></td><td>3 ¦19 4 ¦20</td><td>3 ¦19 4 ¦20</td><td>I</td><td></td><td></td></tr>
<tr><td>II</td><td></td><td></td><td>5 ¦21 6 ¦22</td><td>5 ¦21 6 ¦22</td><td>II</td><td></td><td></td></tr>
<tr><td>III</td><td></td><td></td><td>7 ¦23 8 ¦24</td><td>7 ¦23 8 ¦24</td><td>III</td><td></td><td></td></tr>
<tr><td>IV</td><td></td><td></td><td>9 ¦25 10¦26</td><td>9 ¦25 10¦26</td><td>IV</td><td></td><td></td></tr>
<tr><td>V</td><td></td><td></td><td>11¦27 12¦28</td><td>11¦27 12¦28</td><td>V</td><td></td><td></td></tr>
<tr><td>VI</td><td></td><td></td><td>13¦29 14¦30 15¦31</td><td>13¦29 14¦30 15¦31</td><td>VI</td><td></td><td></td></tr>
<tr><td colspan="3">Substitutions:1 2 3 4 5 6 7 8 9 10 11 12 13 14 15 16 17 18</td><td>16¦32</td><td>16¦32</td><td colspan="3">Substitutions:1 2 3 4 5 6 7 8 9 10 11 12 13 14 15 16 17 18</td></tr>
<tr><td colspan="3">Comments:</td><td colspan="2">Final Score</td><td colspan="3">Comments:</td></tr>
</table>

REFEREE'S VERIFICATION		SCOREKEEPER	
FIRST REFEREE		WINNING TEAM	
SECOND REFEREE		LOSING TEAM	

KEYS:

C = Playing Captain
S = Substitution
Sx = Substitution Opponent

—| = Loss Of Rally
R = Replay
RS = Re-Serve

T = Time-Out
Tx = Time-Out Opponent
1,2,3..etc = General Point

P1, P2, P3 = Penalty Point
Px = Penalty Opponent
▢ = Point Scored Off Loss Of Rally
△ = Libero Point

If the receiving team wins the rally, it receives a point which is recorded on the line of the next server's number and a square is drawn around it. Also draw a square around the same point on the team's running score. Draw a triangle around serve order position in which the Libero serves and around all points score by the Libero.

| Date: | | Location: | | | | | | Start Time: | | Finish Time: | |

| Home Team: | | Visitor Team: | | | | | Game No.: | | Level: | |

| Time-Outs | | TEAM: | | First Serve | | Time-Outs | | TEAM: | |

Left side:

Time-Outs		TEAM:

Serve Order	Player No.	Libero # :
I		
II		
III		
IV		
V		
VI		

Center (First Serve / Running Score):

First Serve

Running Score

1	17	1	17
2	18	2	18
3	19	3	19
4	20	4	20
5	21	5	21
6	22	6	22
7	23	7	23
8	24	8	24
9	25	9	25
10	26	10	26
11	27	11	27
12	28	12	28
13	29	13	29
14	30	14	30
15	31	15	31
16	32	16	32

Final Score

Right side:

Time-Outs		TEAM:

Serve Order	Player No.	Libero # :
I		
II		
III		
IV		
V		
VI		

Substitutions: 1 2 3 4 5 6 7 8 9 10 11 12 13 14 15 16 17 18

Comments:

Substitutions: 1 2 3 4 5 6 7 8 9 10 11 12 13 14 15 16 17 18

Comments:

REFEREE'S VERIFICATION		SCOREKEEPER	
FIRST REFEREE		WINNING TEAM	
SECOND REFEREE		LOSING TEAM	

KEYS:

C = Playing Captain

S = Substitution

Sx = Substitution Opponent

⊣ = Loss Of Rally

R = Replay

RS = Re-Serve

T = Time-Out

Tx = Time-Out Opponent

1,2,3..etc = General Point

P1, P2, P3 = Penalty Point

Px = Penalty Opponent

☐ = Point Scored Off Loss Of Rally

△ = Libero Point

If the receiving team wins the rally, it receives a point which is recorded on the line of the next server's number and a square is drawn around it. Also draw a square around the same point on the team's running score. Draw a triangle around serve order position in which the Libero serves and around all points score by the Libero.

Date:	Location:		Start Time:	Finish Time:
Home Team:	Visitor Team:		Game No.:	Level:

Time-Outs		TEAM:	First Serve	Time-Outs		TEAM:

Serve Order	Player No.	Libero # :	Running Score	Serve Order	Player No.	Libero # :

Running Score:
1 17 1 17
2 18 2 18
3 19 3 19
4 20 4 20
5 21 5 21
6 22 6 22
7 23 7 23
8 24 8 24
9 25 9 25
10 26 10 26
11 27 11 27
12 28 12 28
13 29 13 29
14 30 14 30
15 31 15 31
16 32 16 32

Serve Order (left): I, II, III, IV, V, VI
Serve Order (right): I, II, III, IV, V, VI

Substitutions: 1 2 3 4 5 6 7 8 9 10 11 12 13 14 15 16 17 18

Final Score

Substitutions: 1 2 3 4 5 6 7 8 9 10 11 12 13 14 15 16 17 18

Comments:

Comments:

REFEREE'S VERIFICATION		SCOREKEEPER	
FIRST REFEREE		WINNING TEAM	
SECOND REFEREE		LOSING TEAM	

KEYS:

C = Playing Captain

S = Substitution

Sx = Substitution Opponent

—| = Loss Of Rally

R = Replay

RS = Re-Serve

T = Time-Out

Tx = Time-Out Opponent

1,2,3..etc = General Point

P1, P2, P3 = Penalty Point

Px = Penalty Opponent

☐ = Point Scored Off Loss Of Rally

△ = Libero Point

If the receiving team wins the rally, it receives a point which is recorded on the line of the next server's number and a square is drawn around it. Also draw a square around the same point on the team's running score. Draw a triangle around serve order position in which the Libero serves and around all points score by the Libero.

Date:		Location:			Start Time:		Finish Time:	
Home Team:			Visitor Team:		Game No.:		Level:	

Time-Outs		TEAM:						First Serve		Time-Outs		TEAM:						

Home side

Serve Order	Player No.	Libero # :
I		
II		
III		
IV		
V		
VI		

Running Score (center)

1 ¦ 17	1 ¦ 17	
2 ¦ 18	2 ¦ 18	
3 ¦ 19	3 ¦ 19	
4 ¦ 20	4 ¦ 20	
5 ¦ 21	5 ¦ 21	
6 ¦ 22	6 ¦ 22	
7 ¦ 23	7 ¦ 23	
8 ¦ 24	8 ¦ 24	
9 ¦ 25	9 ¦ 25	
10 ¦ 26	10 ¦ 26	
11 ¦ 27	11 ¦ 27	
12 ¦ 28	12 ¦ 28	
13 ¦ 29	13 ¦ 29	
14 ¦ 30	14 ¦ 30	
15 ¦ 31	15 ¦ 31	
16 ¦ 32	16 ¦ 32	

Visitor side

Serve Order	Player No.	Libero # :
I		
II		
III		
IV		
V		
VI		

Substitutions: 1 2 3 4 5 6 7 8 9 10 11 12 13 14 15 16 17 18

Comments:

Final Score

Substitutions: 1 2 3 4 5 6 7 8 9 10 11 12 13 14 15 16 17 18

Comments:

REFEREE'S VERIFICATION		SCOREKEEPER	
FIRST REFEREE		WINNING TEAM	
SECOND REFEREE		LOSING TEAM	

KEYS:

C = Playing Captain
S = Substitution
Sx = Substitution Opponent
━| = Loss Of Rally
R = Replay
RS = Re-Serve
T = Time-Out
Tx = Time-Out Opponent
1,2,3..etc = General Point
P1, P2, P3 = Penalty Point
Px = Penalty Opponent
☐ = Point Scored Off Loss Of Rally
△ = Libero Point

If the receiving team wins the rally, it receives a point which is recorded on the line of the next server's number and a square is drawn around it. Also draw a square around the same point on the team's running score. Draw a triangle around serve order position in which the Libero serves and around all points score by the Libero.

Date:	Location:		Start Time:	Finish Time:
Home Team:	Visitor Team:		Game No.:	Level:

Time-Outs		TEAM:	First Serve	Time-Outs		TEAM:

Running Score

Serve Order	Player No.	Libero # :		Serve Order	Player No.	Libero # :

Running Score: 1 17 1 17 | 2 18 2 18 | 3 19 3 19 | 4 20 4 20 | 5 21 5 21 | 6 22 6 22 | 7 23 7 23 | 8 24 8 24 | 9 25 9 25 | 10 26 10 26 | 11 27 11 27 | 12 28 12 28 | 13 29 13 29 | 14 30 14 30 | 15 31 15 31 | 16 32 16 32

Serve Order rows: I, II, III, IV, V, VI

Substitutions: 1 2 3 4 5 6 7 8 9 10 11 12 13 14 15 16 17 18

Comments:

Final Score

Substitutions: 1 2 3 4 5 6 7 8 9 10 11 12 13 14 15 16 17 18

Comments:

REFEREE'S VERIFICATION		SCOREKEEPER	
FIRST REFEREE		WINNING TEAM	
SECOND REFEREE		LOSING TEAM	

KEYS:

C = Playing Captain
S = Substitution
Sx = Substitution Opponent

⊣ = Loss Of Rally
R = Replay
RS = Re-Serve

T = Time-Out
Tx = Time-Out Opponent
1,2,3..etc = General Point

P1, P2, P3 = Penalty Point
Px = Penalty Opponent
☐ = Point Scored Off Loss Of Rally
△ = Libero Point

If the receiving team wins the rally, it receives a point which is recorded on the line of the next server's number and a square is drawn around it. Also draw a square around the same point on the team's running score. Draw a triangle around serve order position in which the Libero serves and around all points score by the Libero.

Date:	Location:		Start Time:	Finish Time:
Home Team:	Visitor Team:		Game No.:	Level:

Time-Outs		TEAM:						First Serve		Time-Outs		TEAM:			

Running Score

Home side — Serve Order / Player No. / Libero # :

Serve Order	Player No.	Libero # :							
I		-------							
II		-------							
III		-------							
IV		-------							
V		-------							
VI		-------							

Running Score columns:

1 : 17	1 : 17
2 : 18	2 : 18
3 : 19	3 : 19
4 : 20	4 : 20
5 : 21	5 : 21
6 : 22	6 : 22
7 : 23	7 : 23
8 : 24	8 : 24
9 : 25	9 : 25
10 : 26	10 : 26
11 : 27	11 : 27
12 : 28	12 : 28
13 : 29	13 : 29
14 : 30	14 : 30
15 : 31	15 : 31
16 : 32	16 : 32

Visitor side — Serve Order / Player No. / Libero # :

Serve Order	Player No.	Libero # :							
I		-------							
II		-------							
III		-------							
IV		-------							
V		-------							
VI		-------							

Substitutions: 1 2 3 4 5 6 7 8 9 10 11 12 13 14 15 16 17 18

Final Score

Substitutions: 1 2 3 4 5 6 7 8 9 10 11 12 13 14 15 16 17 18

Comments:

Comments:

REFEREE'S VERIFICATION		SCOREKEEPER	
FIRST REFEREE		WINNING TEAM	
SECOND REFEREE		LOSING TEAM	

KEYS:

C = Playing Captain
S = Substitution
Sx = Substitution Opponent

—| = Loss Of Rally
R = Replay
RS = Re-Serve

T = Time-Out
Tx = Time-Out Opponent
1,2,3..etc = General Point

P1, P2, P3 = Penalty Point
Px = Penalty Opponent
☐ = Point Scored Off Loss Of Rally
△ = Libero Point

If the receiving team wins the rally, it receives a point which is recorded on the line of the next server's number and a square is drawn around it. Also draw a square around the same point on the team's running score. Draw a triangle around serve order position in which the Libero serves and around all points score by the Libero.

Date:	Location:		Start Time:	Finish Time:

Home Team:	Visitor Team:	Game No.:	Level:

| Time-Outs | TEAM: | First Serve | Time-Outs | TEAM: |

Running Score

Serve Order	Player No.	Libero # :		Serve Order	Player No.	Libero # :
I			1 ¦ 17 1 ¦17 2 ¦ 18 2 ¦18	I		
II			3 ¦ 19 3 ¦19 4 ¦ 20 4 ¦20	II		
III			5 ¦ 21 5 ¦21 6 ¦ 22 6 ¦22	III		
IV			7 ¦ 23 7 ¦23 8 ¦ 24 8 ¦24	IV		
V			9 ¦ 25 9 ¦25 10¦ 26 10¦26 11¦27 11¦27 12¦28 12¦28	V		
VI			13¦29 13¦29 14¦30 14¦30 15¦31 15¦31	VI		

Substitutions: 1 2 3 4 5 6 7 8 9 10 11 12 13 14 15 16 17 18	16¦32 16¦32	Substitutions: 1 2 3 4 5 6 7 8 9 10 11 12 13 14 15 16 17 18
Comments:	Final Score	Comments:

REFEREE'S VERIFICATION		SCOREKEEPER	
FIRST REFEREE		WINNING TEAM	
SECOND REFEREE		LOSING TEAM	

KEYS:

C = Playing Captain
S = Substitution
Sx = Substitution Opponent

▬| = Loss Of Rally
R = Replay
RS = Re-Serve

T = Time-Out
Tx = Time-Out Opponent
1,2,3..etc = General Point

P1, P2, P3 = Penalty Point
Px = Penalty Opponent
☐ = Point Scored Off Loss Of Rally
△ = Libero Point

If the receiving team wins the rally, it receives a point which is recorded on the line of the next server's number and a square is drawn around it. Also draw a square around the same point on the team's running score. Draw a triangle around serve order position in which the Libero serves and around all points score by the Libero.

| Date: | | Location: | | | | Start Time: | | Finish Time: | |

| Home Team: | | Visitor Team: | | | Game No.: | | Level: | |

<table>
<tr><td colspan="2">Time-Outs</td><td rowspan="2">TEAM:</td><td></td><td></td><td></td><td></td><td></td><td colspan="2">First Serve</td><td colspan="2">Time-Outs</td><td rowspan="2">TEAM:</td><td></td></tr>
<tr><td></td><td></td><td></td><td></td><td></td><td></td><td></td><td colspan="2">Running Score</td><td></td><td></td><td></td></tr>
</table>

Time-Outs | **TEAM:** | | | **First Serve** | | **Time-Outs** | **TEAM:**

Running Score

Serve Order	Player No.	Libero # :								1 : 17	1 : 17	Serve Order	Player No.	Libero # :
I										2 : 18	2 : 18	I		
										3 : 19	3 : 19			
										4 : 20	4 : 20			
II										5 : 21	5 : 21	II		
										6 : 22	6 : 22			
III										7 : 23	7 : 23	III		
										8 : 24	8 : 24			
IV										9 : 25	9 : 25	IV		
										10 : 26	10 : 26			
V										11 : 27	11 : 27	V		
										12 : 28	12 : 28			
										13 : 29	13 : 29			
VI										14 : 30	14 : 30	VI		
										15 : 31	15 : 31			

Substitutions: 1 2 3 4 5 6 7 8 9 10 11 12 13 14 15 16 17 18 | 16 : 32 | 16 : 32 | **Substitutions:** 1 2 3 4 5 6 7 8 9 10 11 12 13 14 15 16 17 18

Comments: | **Final Score** | **Comments:**

REFEREE'S VERIFICATION		**SCOREKEEPER**	
FIRST REFEREE		**WINNING TEAM**	
SECOND REFEREE		**LOSING TEAM**	

KEYS:

C = Playing Captain   —| = Loss Of Rally   T = Time-Out   P1, P2, P3 = Penalty Point

S = Substitution   R = Replay   Tx = Time-Out Opponent   Px = Penalty Opponent

Sx = Substitution Opponent   RS = Re-Serve   1,2,3..etc = General Point   □ = Point Scored Off Loss Of Rally

△ = Libero Point

If the receiving team wins the rally, it receives a point which is recorded on the line of the next server's number and a square is drawn around it. Also draw a square around the same point on the team's running score. Draw a triangle around serve order position in which the Libero serves and around all points score by the Libero.

Date:	Location:		Start Time:	Finish Time:
Home Team:	Visitor Team:		Game No.:	Level:

Time-Outs	TEAM:		First Serve	Time-Outs	TEAM:

Running Score

Serve Order	Player No.	Libero # :		Serve Order	Player No.	Libero # :

1	17	1	17
2	18	2	18
3	19	3	19
4	20	4	20
5	21	5	21
6	22	6	22
7	23	7	23
8	24	8	24
9	25	9	25
10	26	10	26
11	27	11	27
12	28	12	28
13	29	13	29
14	30	14	30
15	31	15	31
16	32	16	32

Serve Order (left): I, II, III, IV, V, VI
Serve Order (right): I, II, III, IV, V, VI

Substitutions: 1 2 3 4 5 6 7 8 9 10 11 12 13 14 15 16 17 18

Substitutions: 1 2 3 4 5 6 7 8 9 10 11 12 13 14 15 16 17 18

Comments:

Final Score

Comments:

REFEREE'S VERIFICATION		SCOREKEEPER	
FIRST REFEREE		WINNING TEAM	
SECOND REFEREE		LOSING TEAM	

KEYS:

C = Playing Captain
S = Substitution
Sx = Substitution Opponent

▬| = Loss Of Rally
R = Replay
RS = Re-Serve

T = Time-Out
Tx = Time-Out Opponent
1,2,3..etc = General Point

P1, P2, P3 = Penalty Point
Px = Penalty Opponent
☐ = Point Scored Off Loss Of Rally
△ = Libero Point

If the receiving team wins the rally, it receives a point which is recorded on the line of the next server's number and a square is drawn around it. Also draw a square around the same point on the team's running score. Draw a triangle around serve order position in which the Libero serves and around all points score by the Libero.

Date:		Location:			Start Time:		Finish Time:	
Home Team:			Visitor Team:		Game No.:		Level:	

Time-Outs		TEAM:			First Serve		Time-Outs		TEAM:	
					Running Score					

Serve Order	Player No.	Libero # :												1	17	1	17	Serve Order	Player No.	Libero # :												
														2	18	2	18															
I														3	19	3	19	I													
														4	20	4	20														
II														5	21	5	21	II													
														6	22	6	22														
III														7	23	7	23	III													
														8	24	8	24														
IV														9	25	9	25	IV													
														10	26	10	26														
														11	27	11	27														
V														12	28	12	28	V													
														13	29	13	29														
VI														14	30	14	30	VI													
														15	31	15	31														

Substitutions: 1 2 3 4 5 6 7 8 9 10 11 12 13 14 15 16 17 18 | 16 32 | 16 32 | Substitutions: 1 2 3 4 5 6 7 8 9 10 11 12 13 14 15 16 17 18

Comments: | Final Score | Comments:

REFEREE'S VERIFICATION		SCOREKEEPER	
FIRST REFEREE		WINNING TEAM	
SECOND REFEREE		LOSING TEAM	

KEYS:

C = Playing Captain
S = Substitution
Sx = Substitution Opponent

⊣ = Loss Of Rally
R = Replay
RS = Re-Serve

T = Time-Out
Tx = Time-Out Opponent
1,2,3..etc = General Point

P1, P2, P3 = Penalty Point
Px = Penalty Opponent
☐ = Point Scored Off Loss Of Rally
△ = Libero Point

If the receiving team wins the rally, it receives a point which is recorded on the line of the next server's number and a square is drawn around it. Also draw a square around the same point on the team's running score. Draw a triangle around serve order position in which the Libero serves and around all points score by the Libero.

Date:	Location:		Start Time:	Finish Time:
Home Team:	Visitor Team:		Game No.:	Level:

Time-Outs		TEAM:	First Serve	Time-Outs		TEAM:
			Running Score			

Serve Order	Player No.	Libero # :								1 17 1 17	Serve Order	Player No.	Libero # :
										2 18 2 18			
I										3 19 3 19	I		
										4 20 4 20			
II										5 21 5 21	II		
										6 22 6 22			
III										7 23 7 23	III		
										8 24 8 24			
IV										9 25 9 25	IV		
										10 26 10 26			
V										11 27 11 27	V		
										12 28 12 28			
VI										13 29 13 29	VI		
										14 30 14 30			
										15 31 15 31			

Substitutions: 1 2 3 4 5 6 7 8 9 10 11 12 13 14 15 16 17 18	16 32 16 32	Substitutions: 1 2 3 4 5 6 7 8 9 10 11 12 13 14 15 16 17 18
Comments:	Final Score	Comments:

REFEREE'S VERIFICATION		SCOREKEEPER	
FIRST REFEREE		WINNING TEAM	
SECOND REFEREE		LOSING TEAM	

KEYS:

C = Playing Captain

S = Substitution

Sx = Substitution Opponent

⊣ = Loss Of Rally

R = Replay

RS = Re-Serve

T = Time-Out

Tx = Time-Out Opponent

1,2,3..etc = General Point

P1, P2, P3 = Penalty Point

Px = Penalty Opponent

☐ = Point Scored Off Loss Of Rally

△ = Libero Point

If the receiving team wins the rally, it receives a point which is recorded on the line of the next server's number and a square is drawn around it. Also draw a square around the same point on the team's running score. Draw a triangle around serve order position in which the Libero serves and around all points score by the Libero.

Date:	Location:		Start Time:	Finish Time:
Home Team:	Visitor Team:		Game No.:	Level:

Time-Outs		TEAM:	First Serve	Time-Outs		TEAM:

Running Score

Serve Order	Player No.	Libero # :									1 17 1 17	Serve Order	Player No.	Libero # :									
											2 18 2 18												
I											3 19 3 19	I											
											4 20 4 20												
II											5 21 5 21	II											
											6 22 6 22												
III											7 23 7 23	III											
											8 24 8 24												
IV											9 25 9 25	IV											
											10 26 10 26												
V											11 27 11 27	V											
											12 28 12 28												
											13 29 13 29												
VI											14 30 14 30	VI											
											15 31 15 31												

Substitutions:1 2 3 4 5 6 7 8 9 10 11 12 13 14 15 16 17 18	16 32 16 32	Substitutions:1 2 3 4 5 6 7 8 9 10 11 12 13 14 15 16 17 18
Comments:	Final Score	Comments:

REFEREE'S VERIFICATION		SCOREKEEPER	
FIRST REFEREE		WINNING TEAM	
SECOND REFEREE		LOSING TEAM	

KEYS:

C = Playing Captain

S = Substitution

Sx = Substitution Opponent

—| = Loss Of Rally

R = Replay

RS = Re-Serve

T = Time-Out

Tx = Time-Out Opponent

1,2,3..etc = General Point

P1, P2, P3 = Penalty Point

Px = Penalty Opponent

☐ = Point Scored Off Loss Of Rally

△ = Libero Point

If the receiving team wins the rally, it receives a point which is recorded on the line of the next server's number and a square is drawn around it. Also draw a square around the same point on the team's running score. Draw a triangle around serve order position in which the Libero serves and around all points score by the Libero.

Date:		Location:					Start Time:		Finish Time:	
Home Team:			Visitor Team:				Game No.:		Level:	

Time-Outs		TEAM:	First Serve		Time-Outs		TEAM:

Serve Order	Player No.	Libero # :	Running Score	Serve Order	Player No.	Libero # :
I			1 17	1 17	I		
			2 18	2 18			
II			3 19	3 19	II		
			4 20	4 20			
III			5 21	5 21	III		
			6 22	6 22			
			7 23	7 23			
			8 24	8 24			
IV			9 25	9 25	IV		
			10 26	10 26			
V			11 27	11 27	V		
			12 28	12 28			
			13 29	13 29			
VI			14 30	14 30	VI		
			15 31	15 31			

Substitutions: 1 2 3 4 5 6 7 8 9 10 11 12 13 14 15 16 17 18 | 16 32 | 16 32 | Substitutions: 1 2 3 4 5 6 7 8 9 10 11 12 13 14 15 16 17 18

Comments: | Final Score | Comments:

REFEREE'S VERIFICATION		SCOREKEEPER	
FIRST REFEREE		WINNING TEAM	
SECOND REFEREE		LOSING TEAM	

KEYS:

C = Playing Captain
S = Substitution
Sx = Substitution Opponent

—| = Loss Of Rally
R = Replay
RS = Re-Serve

T = Time-Out
Tx = Time-Out Opponent
1,2,3..etc = General Point

P1, P2, P3 = Penalty Point
Px = Penalty Opponent
□ = Point Scored Off Loss Of Rally
△ = Libero Point

If the receiving team wins the rally, it receives a point which is recorded on the line of the next server's number and a square is drawn around it. Also draw a square around the same point on the team's running score. Draw a triangle around serve order position in which the Libero serves and around all points score by the Libero.

Date:	Location:		Start Time:	Finish Time:

Home Team:	Visitor Team:	Game No.:	Level:

Time-Outs	TEAM:		First Serve	Time-Outs	TEAM:

Running Score

Serve Order	Player No.	Libero # :											1 17 1 17	Serve Order	Player No.	Libero # :
													2 18 2 18			
I	------												3 19 3 19	I	------	
													4 20 4 20			
II	------												5 21 5 21	II	------	
													6 22 6 22			
III	------												7 23 7 23	III	------	
													8 24 8 24			
IV	------												9 25 9 25	IV	------	
													10 26 10 26			
V	------												11 27 11 27	V	------	
													12 28 12 28			
													13 29 13 29			
VI	------												14 30 14 30	VI	------	
													15 31 15 31			

Substitutions: 1 2 3 4 5 6 7 8 9 10 11 12 13 14 15 16 17 18 | 16 32 16 32 | Substitutions: 1 2 3 4 5 6 7 8 9 10 11 12 13 14 15 16 17 18

Comments: | **Final Score** | Comments:

REFEREE'S VERIFICATION		SCOREKEEPER	
FIRST REFEREE		WINNING TEAM	
SECOND REFEREE		LOSING TEAM	

KEYS:

C = Playing Captain ⊣ = Loss Of Rally T = Time-Out P1, P2, P3 = Penalty Point

S = Substitution R = Replay Tx = Time-Out Opponent Px = Penalty Opponent

Sx = Substitution Opponent RS = Re-Serve 1,2,3..etc = General Point ☐ = Point Scored Off Loss Of Rally

△ = Libero Point

If the receiving team wins the rally, it receives a point which is recorded on the line of the next server's number and a square is drawn around it. Also draw a square around the same point on the team's running score. Draw a triangle around serve order position in which the Libero serves and around all points score by the Libero.

Date:	Location:		Start Time:	Finish Time:

Home Team:	Visitor Team:	Game No.:	Level:

Time-Outs		TEAM:		First Serve		Time-Outs		TEAM:	
				Running Score					

Serve Order	Player No.	Libero # :											First Serve		Serve Order	Player No.	Libero # :										
													1 17	1 17														
													2 18	2 18														
I													3 19	3 19	I													
													4 20	4 20														
II													5 21	5 21	II													
													6 22	6 22														
III													7 23	7 23	III													
													8 24	8 24														
IV													9 25	9 25	IV													
													10 26	10 26														
V													11 27	11 27	V													
													12 28	12 28														
													13 29	13 29														
VI													14 30	14 30	VI													
													15 31	15 31														

Substitutions: 1 2 3 4 5 6 7 8 9 10 11 12 13 14 15 16 17 18 | 16 32 | 16 32 | Substitutions: 1 2 3 4 5 6 7 8 9 10 11 12 13 14 15 16 17 18

Comments: | Final Score | Comments:

REFEREE'S VERIFICATION		SCOREKEEPER	
FIRST REFEREE		WINNING TEAM	
SECOND REFEREE		LOSING TEAM	

KEYS:

C = Playing Captain   ⊣ = Loss Of Rally   T = Time-Out   P1, P2, P3 = Penalty Point

S = Substitution   R = Replay   Tx = Time-Out Opponent   Px = Penalty Opponent

Sx = Substitution Opponent   RS = Re-Serve   1,2,3..etc = General Point   ☐ = Point Scored Off Loss Of Rally

△ = Libero Point

If the receiving team wins the rally, it receives a point which is recorded on the line of the next server's number and a square is drawn around it. Also draw a square around the same point on the team's running score. Draw a triangle around serve order position in which the Libero serves and around all points score by the Libero.

Date:		Location:						Start Time:		Finish Time:	

Home Team:		Visitor Team:			Game No.:		Level:	

Time-Outs		TEAM:						First Serve		Time-Outs		TEAM:	

| Serve Order | Player No. | Libero # : | | | | | | | Running Score | | Serve Order | Player No. | Libero # : |

Running Score columns:

1	17	1	17
2	18	2	18
3	19	3	19
4	20	4	20
5	21	5	21
6	22	6	22
7	23	7	23
8	24	8	24
9	25	9	25
10	26	10	26
11	27	11	27
12	28	12	28
13	29	13	29
14	30	14	30
15	31	15	31
16	32	16	32

Serve Order positions (left team): I, II, III, IV, V, VI
Serve Order positions (right team): I, II, III, IV, V, VI

Substitutions: 1 2 3 4 5 6 7 8 9 10 11 12 13 14 15 16 17 18

Comments:

Final Score

Substitutions: 1 2 3 4 5 6 7 8 9 10 11 12 13 14 15 16 17 18

Comments:

REFEREE'S VERIFICATION		SCOREKEEPER	
FIRST REFEREE		WINNING TEAM	
SECOND REFEREE		LOSING TEAM	

KEYS:

C = Playing Captain
S = Substitution
Sx = Substitution Opponent

—| = Loss Of Rally
R = Replay
RS = Re-Serve

T = Time-Out
Tx = Time-Out Opponent
1,2,3..etc = General Point

P1, P2, P3 = Penalty Point
Px = Penalty Opponent
☐ = Point Scored Off Loss Of Rally
△ = Libero Point

If the receiving team wins the rally, it receives a point which is recorded on the line of the next server's number and a square is drawn around it. Also draw a square around the same point on the team's running score. Draw a triangle around serve order position in which the Libero serves and around all points score by the Libero.

| Date: | | Location: | | | | | | Start Time: | | Finish Time: | | |

| Home Team: | | | Visitor Team: | | | | | Game No.: | | Level: | | |

Time-Outs		TEAM:				First Serve		Time-Outs		TEAM:		
						Running Score						

Serve Order	Player No.	Libero # :				1 17	1 17	Serve Order	Player No.	Libero # :		
						2 18	2 18					
I						3 19	3 19	I				
						4 20	4 20					
II						5 21	5 21	II				
						6 22	6 22					
III						7 23	7 23	III				
						8 24	8 24					
IV						9 25	9 25	IV				
						10 26	10 26					
V						11 27	11 27	V				
						12 28	12 28					
						13 29	13 29					
VI						14 30	14 30	VI				
						15 31	15 31					

Substitutions: 1 2 3 4 5 6 7 8 9 10 11 12 13 14 15 16 17 18 | 16 32 | 16 32 | Substitutions: 1 2 3 4 5 6 7 8 9 10 11 12 13 14 15 16 17 18

Comments: | Final Score | Comments:

REFEREE'S VERIFICATION		SCOREKEEPER	
FIRST REFEREE		WINNING TEAM	
SECOND REFEREE		LOSING TEAM	

KEYS:

C = Playing Captain
S = Substitution
Sx = Substitution Opponent

▬| = Loss Of Rally
R = Replay
RS = Re-Serve

T = Time-Out
Tx = Time-Out Opponent
1,2,3..etc = General Point

P1, P2, P3 = Penalty Point
Px = Penalty Opponent
□ = Point Scored Off Loss Of Rally
△ = Libero Point

If the receiving team wins the rally, it receives a point which is recorded on the line of the next server's number and a square is drawn around it. Also draw a square around the same point on the team's running score. Draw a triangle around serve order position in which the Libero serves and around all points score by the Libero.

| Date: | Location: | | Start Time: | Finish Time: |

| Home Team: | Visitor Team: | | Game No.: | Level: |

<table>
<tr><td colspan="2">Time-Outs</td><td rowspan="2">TEAM:</td><td colspan="2">First Serve</td><td colspan="2">Time-Outs</td><td rowspan="2">TEAM:</td></tr>
<tr><td></td><td></td><td colspan="2">Running Score</td><td></td><td></td></tr>
<tr><td>Serve Order</td><td>Player No.</td><td>Libero # :</td><td>1 ¦ 17
2 ¦ 18</td><td>1 ¦ 17
2 ¦ 18</td><td>Serve Order</td><td>Player No.</td><td>Libero # :</td></tr>
<tr><td>I</td><td></td><td>-------</td><td>3 ¦ 19
4 ¦ 20</td><td>3 ¦ 19
4 ¦ 20</td><td>I</td><td></td><td>-------</td></tr>
<tr><td>II</td><td></td><td>-------</td><td>5 ¦ 21
6 ¦ 22</td><td>5 ¦ 21
6 ¦ 22</td><td>II</td><td></td><td>-------</td></tr>
<tr><td>III</td><td></td><td>-------</td><td>7 ¦ 23
8 ¦ 24</td><td>7 ¦ 23
8 ¦ 24</td><td>III</td><td></td><td>-------</td></tr>
<tr><td>IV</td><td></td><td>-------</td><td>9 ¦ 25
10 ¦ 26</td><td>9 ¦ 25
10 ¦ 26</td><td>IV</td><td></td><td>-------</td></tr>
<tr><td>V</td><td></td><td>-------</td><td>11 ¦ 27
12 ¦ 28</td><td>11 ¦ 27
12 ¦ 28</td><td>V</td><td></td><td>-------</td></tr>
<tr><td>VI</td><td></td><td>-------</td><td>13 ¦ 29
14 ¦ 30
15 ¦ 31</td><td>13 ¦ 29
14 ¦ 30
15 ¦ 31</td><td>VI</td><td></td><td>-------</td></tr>
<tr><td colspan="2">Substitutions:</td><td>1 2 3 4 5 6 7 8 9 10 11 12 13 14 15 16 17 18</td><td>16 ¦ 32</td><td>16 ¦ 32</td><td colspan="2">Substitutions:</td><td>1 2 3 4 5 6 7 8 9 10 11 12 13 14 15 16 17 18</td></tr>
<tr><td colspan="2">Comments:</td><td></td><td colspan="2">Final Score</td><td colspan="2">Comments:</td><td></td></tr>
</table>

REFEREE'S VERIFICATION		SCOREKEEPER	
FIRST REFEREE		WINNING TEAM	
SECOND REFEREE		LOSING TEAM	

KEYS:

C = Playing Captain

S = Substitution

Sx = Substitution Opponent

—| = Loss Of Rally

R = Replay

RS = Re-Serve

T = Time-Out

Tx = Time-Out Opponent

1,2,3..etc = General Point

P1, P2, P3 = Penalty Point

Px = Penalty Opponent

□ = Point Scored Off Loss Of Rally

△ = Libero Point

If the receiving team wins the rally, it receives a point which is recorded on the line of the next server's number and a square is drawn around it. Also draw a square around the same point on the team's running score. Draw a triangle around serve order position in which the Libero serves and around all points score by the Libero.

Date:	Location:		Start Time:	Finish Time:
Home Team:	Visitor Team:		Game No.:	Level:

Time-Outs	TEAM:		First Serve	Time-Outs	TEAM:

			Running Score		

Serve Order	Player No.	Libero # :		Serve Order	Player No.	Libero # :

First Serve running score columns:

1	17	1	17
2	18	2	18
3	19	3	19
4	20	4	20
5	21	5	21
6	22	6	22
7	23	7	23
8	24	8	24
9	25	9	25
10	26	10	26
11	27	11	27
12	28	12	28
13	29	13	29
14	30	14	30
15	31	15	31
16	32	16	32

Serve Order (left team): I, II, III, IV, V, VI
Serve Order (right team): I, II, III, IV, V, VI

Final Score

Substitutions: 1 2 3 4 5 6 7 8 9 10 11 12 13 14 15 16 17 18

Substitutions: 1 2 3 4 5 6 7 8 9 10 11 12 13 14 15 16 17 18

Comments:

Comments:

REFEREE'S VERIFICATION		SCOREKEEPER	
FIRST REFEREE		WINNING TEAM	
SECOND REFEREE		LOSING TEAM	

KEYS:

C = Playing Captain
S = Substitution
Sx = Substitution Opponent

—| = Loss Of Rally
R = Replay
RS = Re-Serve

T = Time-Out
Tx = Time-Out Opponent
1,2,3..etc = General Point

P1, P2, P3 = Penalty Point
Px = Penalty Opponent
☐ = Point Scored Off Loss Of Rally
△ = Libero Point

If the receiving team wins the rally, it receives a point which is recorded on the line of the next server's number and a square is drawn around it. Also draw a square around the same point on the team's running score. Draw a triangle around serve order position in which the Libero serves and around all points score by the Libero.

| Date: | Location: | | Start Time: | Finish Time: |

| Home Team: | Visitor Team: | Game No.: | Level: |

Time-Outs	TEAM:								First Serve		Time-Outs	TEAM:								
									Running Score												

First Serve / Running Score column:

Serve Order	Player No.	Libero # :	Serve Order	Player No.	Libero # :
I			1 : 17 1 : 17	I	
			2 : 18 2 : 18		
II			3 : 19 3 : 19	II	
			4 : 20 4 : 20		
			5 : 21 5 : 21		
III			6 : 22 6 : 22	III	
			7 : 23 7 : 23		
			8 : 24 8 : 24		
IV			9 : 25 9 : 25	IV	
			10 : 26 10 : 26		
V			11 : 27 11 : 27	V	
			12 : 28 12 : 28		
			13 : 29 13 : 29		
VI			14 : 30 14 : 30	VI	
			15 : 31 15 : 31		

Substitutions:1 2 3 4 5 6 7 8 9 10 11 12 13 14 15 16 17 18 | 16 : 32 16 : 32 | Substitutions:1 2 3 4 5 6 7 8 9 10 11 12 13 14 15 16 17 18

Comments: | Final Score | Comments:

REFEREE'S VERIFICATION		SCOREKEEPER	
FIRST REFEREE		WINNING TEAM	
SECOND REFEREE		LOSING TEAM	

KEYS:

C = Playing Captain
S = Substitution
Sx = Substitution Opponent

—| = Loss Of Rally
R = Replay
RS = Re-Serve

T = Time-Out
Tx = Time-Out Opponent
1,2,3..etc = General Point

P1, P2, P3 = Penalty Point
Px = Penalty Opponent
☐ = Point Scored Off Loss Of Rally
△ = Libero Point

If the receiving team wins the rally, it receives a point which is recorded on the line of the next server's number and a square is drawn around it. Also draw a square around the same point on the team's running score. Draw a triangle around serve order position in which the Libero serves and around all points score by the Libero.

Made in the USA
Las Vegas, NV
28 September 2024